ITALIAN COOKING SCHOOL

VEGETABLES

ITALIAN COOKING SCHOOL

VEGETABLES

THE SILVER SPOON KITCHEN

EAT YOUR GREENS

Vegetables are an essential part of a balanced and healthy diet. The nutrients in vegetables help us feel energized and are essential in the maintenance of the body. They also reduce the risk of chronic diseases, such as heart disease, high blood pressure, and some cancers. As more and more nutritionists and chefs extol the virtues of plant-base diets, home cooks are discovering that vegetables no longer play supporting roles to rich, protein-base main courses. In fact, they can be the highlight of a meal.

From simple salads, such as Avocado Salad (page 27) to tried-and-true classics like Eggplant Parmesan (page 140), *Italian Cooking School Vegetables* features our favorite vegetable recipes from the Silver Spoon archives. As with all the titles in the series, the book is organized by techniques and guided by popular cooking methods. Each chapter begins with a simple recipe accompanied by step-by-step techniques and is followed by a collection of recipes designed to inspire.

Fresh vegetables are an integral part of the Italian diet and the Italians have always recognized the values of eating seasonally. While most vegetables are available year round, we encourage you to buy yours in season when the produce has been harvested at the height of ripeness and taste their best.

Italian Cooking School Vegetables is a practical, straightforward guide to preparing tasty, nourishing vegetable dishes for family and friends. Eating your vegetables can truly be a pleasure.

INGREDIENTS

ROOT VEGETABLES	These vegetables have a high moisture content and nutritional value. The beet's (beetroot's) large root is cooked before it is eaten and contains a natural colorant. Root vegetables include turnips, carrots (with a high content of beta-carotene), radishes, black salsify, celeriac, and horseradish.

BULB VEGETABLES	Bulb vegetables include garlic, onion, shallot, scallion (spring onion), leek, and tassel hyacinth bulbs (wild baby onions). These vegetables have a strong and distinctive flavor due to their content of allyl sulfur. They have always formed part of the Italian diet but are also valued for their medicinal properties.

BUD VEGETABLES	There is a wide variety of these types of vegetables, which are eaten before they mature. These include Brussels sprouts, capers, and asparagus.

FRUITING VEGETABLES	These vegetables are the fruits (or berries) of herbaceous plants, including climbing or creeping vegetables, such as tomatoes, eggplant (aubergine), cucumber, pumpkin, and other squash. Some are fleshy, some hollow, and some segmented. They are highly nutritious and contain high levels of vitamins A and C.

FLOWERING VEGETABLES	The flowers, and sometimes the leaves, of these are eaten. They have a high fiber content and plenty of vitamin C (except for artichokes). Examples include cauliflower, Brussels sprouts, broccoli, artichokes, green cabbage heads, savoy cabbage, and turnip greens (tops).

GREENS OR LEAVES	Greens (salads)—including Swiss chard (which must always been cooked) and spinach—have a high content of folic acid, vitamins A, C, and K.
STEM OR STALK VEGETABLES	These vegetables usually have a high water content and include asparagus (which can also be included in the category of buds), fennel, and celery (these last two have virtually no calorific content).
TUBERS	Tubers include potatoes (having larger starch granules than those present in cereals, necessitating cooking to make them digestible), cassava (processed to make tapioca, a starchy food with a high nutritional content and used to made baby foods), Jerusalem artichokes, and sweet potatoes. These swollen underground stems (stalks) possess the capability of sustaining new shoots. This means they must contain a store of "energy" that is released by the starch invariably present in this type of vegetable.
LEGUMES	Legumes (pulses), or fruit or seed vegetables, contain a lot of nutrients including 20 percent protein, about 50 percent glucides, 1–2 percent lipids, 10–13 percent water, and vitamins and mineral salts. This means that they provide a complete and healthy food. The main legumes are beans (green [French] beans are classified as vegetables), peas, lentils, fava (broad) beans, chickpeas, black-eyed peas (beans), lupin seeds (*Lupinus luteus*), and soybeans (which consists of 37 percent protein, but also a high lipid content, about 20 percent, hence their use to make oil). Before cooking, soak these legumes in a bowl of water for 12–24 hours, then drain.

COOKING METHODS

There are a number of basic methods of cooking, and they are often divided into two general groups: dry heat and moist heat cooking.

STEAMING

Steaming is one of the best cooking methods for preserving taste and color, while retaining the most nutrients in vegetables. To steam food, fill the bottom of the steamer with 2 inches/5 cm of water. Bring the water to a boil before adding the vegetables to the steamer basket to make sure there is consistent heat throughout the cooking time.

BOILING

Boiling is the most common method of cooking and is also the simplest. Water is heated to near its boiling point, then the food is immersed to cook through. During the heating process, the nutrients can be lost or destroyed and the flavor can be reduced—for example, if cabbage is overcooked, all nutrients can be lost.

STEWING

This is the process of cooking food in a minimum amount of liquid (water, broth/stock, or sauce). The food and the cooking liquid are served together. To avoid overcooking vegetables (and thus increase nutrient loss), vegetables with longer cooking times should be put first into the saucepan, then the ones that need least cooking—such as leafy vegetables—should be put in last.

FRYING

This process uses oil or solid fat to cook vegetables. There are two types of frying: pan-frying (shallow frying) and deep-frying.

ROASTING

One of the easiest methods of cooking, roasting uses dry heat, or hot air, to cook the food evenly on all sides with temperatures of at least 300°F/150°C/Gas Mark 2. Very little nutrients are lost in this process.

BAKING

Like roasting, baking uses prolonged dry heat or hot air—usually an oven—to cook food. Whereas roasting involves cooking foods that are already solid in structure before the cooking process begins; baking often lacks structure and generally becomes solid during this process.

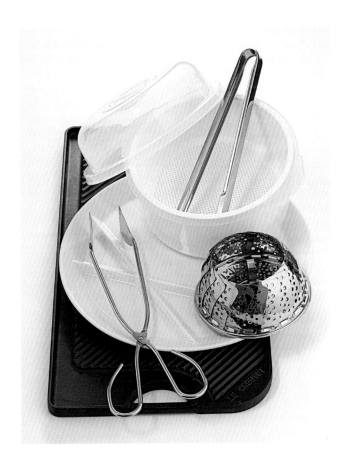

COOKING METHODS

SALADS

HONEY MUSTARD DRESSING

HERB DRESSING

TOMATO PESTO

BALSAMIC DRESSING

EASY

– Preparation time: *10 minutes*
– Calories per serving: *varies*
– *Serves 4*

FOR THE HONEY
MUSTARD DRESSING

– 1 teaspoon mustard
– 1 tablespoon apple cider
  vinegar
– 1 teaspoon honey
– scant ½ cup (3½ fl oz/
  100 ml) extra-virgin olive oil
– salt and pepper

FOR THE
HERB DRESSING

– juice of ½ lemon
– 1 sprig of thyme
– 3–4 chives
– 3 tablespoons extra-virgin
  olive oil
– salt and pepper

FOR THE
TOMATO PESTO

– 2 sun-dried tomatoes,
  drained, dried and diced
– juice of ½ orange
– 1 bunch basil
– 3 tablespoons extra-virgin
  olive oil
– salt and pepper

HONEY MUSTARD DRESSING

To make the honey mustard dressing, combine the mustard, apple cider vinegar, honey, and a pinch of salt. Mix well, then gradually add the oil and whisk thoroughly until emulsified.

HERB DRESSING

Strain the lemon juice, then combine all the ingredients together and whisk thoroughly until emulsified.

TOMATO PESTO

Combine the sun-dried tomatoes and juice in a small bowl. In a separate bowl, combine a handful of basil leaves, a pinch of salt, and oil. Pour the tomato and orange juice mixture into the bowl and whisk well until emulsified.

BALSAMIC DRESSING

Another option is the light balsamic dressing. In a small bowl, combine 1 tablespoon balsamic vinegar, 1 tablespoon Parmesan and 3 tablespoons (2 fl oz/ 50 ml) extra-virgin olive oil and whisk thoroughly until emulsified. Season with salt and pepper.

INSALATA DI POMODORINI MARINATI
MARINATED CHERRY TOMATO SALAD

EASY

– Preparation time: *15 minutes
+ 2 hours chilling*
– Calories per serving: *406*
– *Serves 2*

INGREDIENTS

– 1⅓ cups (7 oz/200 g) halved
cherry tomatoes
– 1 stalk celery, thinly sliced
– 5–6 tablespoons extra-virgin
olive oil
– 1 canned anchovy fillet,
drained and finely chopped
– 1 teaspoon lemon juice
– 1 strip finely pared lemon
rind
– 1 tablespoon chopped fresh
oregano or 1 teaspoon dried
oregano
– 1 clove garlic, thinly sliced
– salt and pepper

Put the tomatoes into a large bowl and add the celery heart. Pour the oil into another bowl, add the anchovy fillet, lemon juice, lemon rind, oregano, and garlic, and season with salt and pepper. Whisk together with a fork, then pour the dressing over the tomato salad. Stir, cover with plastic wrap (clingfilm), and chill in the refrigerator for at least 2 hours. Remove the lemon rind and bring back to room temperature before serving.

INSALATA DEL CONTADINO
FARMER'S SALAD

EASY

– Preparation time: *10 minutes*
– Calories per serving: *458*
– *Serves 4*

INGREDIENTS

– 2½ cups (1 lb 2 oz/500 g)
  cooked fingerling potatoes,
  halved
– 1⅔ cups (7 oz/200 g) cooked
  green (French) beans
– ¾ cup (7 oz/200 g) cooked
  or canned and drained
  cranberry (borlotti) beans
– 1 small onion, thinly sliced
  into rings
– 2 tablespoons white wine
  vinegar
– 6 tablespoons extra-virgin
  olive oil
– 4–6 fresh basil leaves, torn
– salt

Mix the potatoes, green (French) beans, and cranberry (borlotti) beans together in a serving dish and sprinkle with the onion rings.

Pour the vinegar into a bowl and whisk in a generous pinch of salt. Add the olive oil and whisk well again. Pour the dressing over the salad, sprinkle with the basil, and serve.

CETRIOLI ALLE OLIVE
CUCUMBERS WITH OLIVES

EASY

– Preparation time: *25 minutes*
  + 30 minutes standing
– Calories per serving: *81*
– *Serves 4*

INGREDIENTS

– 2 cucumbers, peeled and
  thinly sliced
– 1 tablespoon chopped fresh
  dill
– 1 tablespoon lemon juice,
  strained
– 1 tablespoon extra-virgin
  olive oil
– 20 black olives, pitted and
  quartered
– salt

Put the cucumber slices into a colander, sprinkle with salt, and let stand for 30 minutes. Rinse, drain, pat dry, and put into a salad bowl. Sprinkle with the dill and drizzle with the lemon juice and olive oil. Add the olives, season with salt, if necessary, and toss. Let stand for a few minutes, then serve.

CUORI DI LATTUGA ALLE ERBE
LETTUCE HEARTS WITH HERBS

EASY

– Preparation time: *15 minutes
+ 10 minutes standing*
– Calories per serving: *202*
– *Serves 4*

INGREDIENTS

– 4 romaine (cos) lettuce
hearts
– 1 tablespoon Dijon mustard
– 2 tablespoons balsamic
vinegar
– 5–6 tablespoons extra-virgin
olive oil
– 1 sprig fresh tarragon,
chopped
– 4 fresh chives, chopped
– 1 sprig fresh chervil,
chopped
– salt and pepper

Cut each lettuce heart into halves and put into a salad bowl. Combine the mustard and vinegar in a bowl and season with salt and pepper. Gradually whisk in the olive oil. Sprinkle the lettuce with the herbs and pour the dressing over the salad. Toss and let the flavors mingle for 10 minutes before serving.

INSALATA DI AVOCADO
AVOCADO SALAD

EASY

– Preparation time: *25 minutes*
– Calories per serving: *440*
– *Serves 4*

INGREDIENTS

– 2 avocados
– juice of 1 lemon, strained
– 1 romaine (cos) lettuce,
  separated into leaves
– 2 tomatoes, sliced
– 1 scallion (spring onion),
  sliced
– 2 mandarins or tangerines,
  peeled, pith removed, and
  cut into round slices
– 2 tablespoons chopped fresh
  flat-leaf parsley
– 2 teaspoons Dijon mustard
– 6 tablespoons extra-virgin
  olive oil
– salt and pepper

Peel, halve, and pit the avocados, then cut them into slices and sprinkle with the lemon juice to prevent discoloration. Arrange the lettuce leaves on serving plates.

Make a layer of tomato and scallion (spring onion) slices on the leaves, cover with the avocado slices in a circle, and top with the mandarin slices. Sprinkle with the parsley.

Whisk the mustard, oil, a pinch of salt and pepper together in a bowl, then pour over the salads and serve.

SEDANO ALLE NOCI
CELERY AND WALNUT SALAD

– Preparation time: *25 minutes*
– Calories per serving: *420*
– *Serves 4*

INGREDIENTS

– 3 white celery stalks,
  trimmed
– 1 green apple, peeled, cored,
  and diced
– juice of 1 lemon, strained
– 4 oz/120 g low-fat tomino or
  fontina cheese, diced
– 1 tablespoon chopped fresh
  flat-leaf parsley
– ½ cup (2¾ oz/75 g) chopped
  walnuts
– 5 tablespoons extra-virgin
  olive oil
– salt and pepper

Halve the celery stalks lengthwise and cut into thin strips. Put the celery and apple into a salad bowl and stir in half the lemon juice. Add the cheese, parsley, and half the chopped walnuts.

Whisk the olive oil and remaining lemon juice together in a small bowl and season with salt and pepper. Stir in the remaining walnuts and pour the dressing over the salad.

INSALATA DI CRESCIONE E MELANZANE
WATERCRESS AND EGGPLANT SALAD

EASY

– Preparation time: *15 minutes
+ 10 minutes cooling*
– Cooking time: *8–10 minutes*
– Calories per serving: *227*
– *Serves 6*

INGREDIENTS

– 4 eggplants (aubergines),
peeled and sliced
– 6 tablespoons olive oil, plus
extra for brushing
– 7 oz/200 g watercress
– 1 red bell pepper, seeded
and cut into strips
– 1 clove garlic
– 2 tablespoons white wine
vinegar
– 1 sprig fresh flat-leaf parsley,
chopped
– 3–4 fresh mint leaves,
chopped
– salt

Preheat the broiler (grill). Brush the eggplant (aubergine) slices with oil and broil (grill) for 8–10 minutes, turning once, then cool.

Chop the eggplant slices and put them into a salad bowl with the watercress, bell pepper, and whole garlic clove.

Whisk the vinegar, oil, parsley, and mint leaves together in a bowl, season with salt, and pour the dressing over the salad. Toss lightly, adjust seasoning, and remove the garlic clove before serving.

INSALATA DI LATTUGA, AVOCADO E PEPERONI

LETTUCE, AVOCADO, AND BELL PEPPER SALAD

EASY

– Preparation time: *15 minutes*
– Calories per serving: *180*
– *Serves 4*

INGREDIENTS

– 1 ripe avocado, peeled,
  halved, pitted, and thinly
  sliced
– juice of ½ lemon, strained
– 5 tablespoons olive oil
– 2 teaspoons strong mustard
– 1 large romaine (cos) lettuce
  heart, leaves separated
– 1 small red bell pepper,
  seeded and cut into
  matchsticks
– salt

Put the avocado slices into a bowl and sprinkle with lemon juice to prevent discoloration.

Whisk the olive oil, mustard, and a pinch of salt together in a bowl. Put the lettuce leaves, bell peppers, and avocado slices into a serving dish, pour over the dressing, and serve.

INSALATA RICCA
RICH SALAD

EASY

– Preparation time: *25 minutes*
– Calories per serving: *413*
– *Serves 4*

INGREDIENTS

– 1 avocado
– juice of 1 lemon, strained
– 1 head frisée (curly chicory),
  chopped
– 1 head radicchio, cut into
  strips
– ⅓ cup (1½ oz/40 g) pine
  nuts
– 2 cups (11 oz/300 g) canned
  hearts of palm, drained,
  rinsed,
  and sliced
– 4 tablespoons olive oil
– 1 teaspoon Worcestershire
  sauce
– salt and pepper

Peel, halve, and pit the avocado, then slice thinly and sprinkle with a little of the lemon juice. Put the avocado slices, frisée (curly chicory), radicchio, pine nuts, and palm hearts into a salad bowl.

Whisk the olive oil, Worcestershire sauce, and remaining lemon juice together in a bowl and season with salt and pepper. Pour the dressing over the salad, toss, and serve.

INSALATA SOLARE
SUNSHINE SALAD

EASY

– Preparation time: *15 minutes + 30 minutes standing*
– Calories per serving: *254*
– *Serves 4*

INGREDIENTS

– 1 eggplant (aubergine), peeled and diced
– 6 tablespoons extra-virgin olive oil, plus extra for drizzling
– 1 green bell pepper, seeded and sliced
– 1 red bell pepper, seeded and sliced
– 1 tomato, thinly sliced (optional)
– ½ cup (3½ oz/100 g) green olives, pitted
– 3 tablespoons capers, rinsed and drained
– 1 fresh red chile, seeded and chopped
– salt and pepper

Put the eggplant (aubergine) into a colander, sprinkle with salt, and let stand for 30 minutes. Rinse, pat dry with paper towels, and put it into a salad bowl. Drizzle with olive oil and arrange the green and red bell pepper slices on top. If using, pat the tomato slices dry with paper towels and put them on top of the bell peppers. Sprinkle the olives, capers, and chile over the salad.

Put the olive oil in a bowl, season with salt and pepper, and pour over the salad. Toss just before serving.

Tip: The salad may be dressed 30 minutes beforehand.

INSALATA DI ZUCCHINE NOVELLE
BABY ZUCCHINI SALAD

EASY

– Preparation time: *15 minutes*
  + 30 minutes standing
– Calories per serving: *165*
– *Serves 4*

INGREDIENTS

– 6 baby zucchini (courgettes),
  thinly sliced
– 2 oz/50 g Parmesan cheese,
  shaved
– 1 pinch dried oregano
– 3 tablespoons extra-virgin
  olive oil
– 2 tomatoes, skinned and
  sliced
– salt and pepper

Put the zucchini (courgettes) into a salad bowl, add the Parmesan cheese, oregano, and olive oil and season with salt and pepper. Mix well and let stand in a cool place for at least 30 minutes to let the flavors mingle. Add the tomatoes and mix again just before serving.

INSALATA DI FUNGHI E PINOLI
MUSHROOM AND PINE NUT SALAD

AVERAGE

– Preparation time: *30 minutes*
– Cooking time: *10 minutes*
– Calories per serving: *465–372*
– *Serves 8–10*

INGREDIENTS

– 7 oz/200 g mixed salad
  greens (leaves), such as
  romaine (cos) lettuce,
  frisée, radicchio, and
  Belgian endive (chicory),
  separated into leaves,
  well chilled
– ½ cup (4 fl oz/120 ml)
  extra-virgin olive oil
– 1 clove garlic, lightly crushed
– 1 lb/450 g porcini (cep)
  mushrooms, thinly sliced
– scant ½ cup (2 oz/50 g)
  pine nuts
– 3 tablespoons raspberry
  vinegar
– 7 oz/200 g Brie cheese, diced
– salt and pepper
– fresh basil leaves, to garnish

Transfer the greens (salad leaves) to a salad bowl.

Heat half the oil in a skillet or frying pan with the garlic clove and cook over low heat for 1 minute or until the garlic is lightly browned, then remove and discard it. Add the mushrooms and cook over medium-high heat, stirring occasionally, for 5 minutes. Remove the mushrooms from the pan and set aside.

Add the pine nuts to the pan and cook for another 2–3 minutes, until toasted. Transfer to a bowl.

Pour the remaining oil into the same skillet, carefully add the raspberry vinegar, and season with salt and pepper. Heat quickly, taste, and add a little more raspberry vinegar, if necessary.

Add the mushrooms and pine nuts to the salad, then drizzle the vinaigrette over the salad. Sprinkle with the diced cheese, garnish with basil leaves, and serve.

RAVANELLI IN INSALATA CON LE OLIVE

RADISH SALAD WITH OLIVES

EASY

– Preparation time: *20 minutes*
  + 10 minutes standing
– Calories per serving: *89*
– *Serves 4*

INGREDIENTS

– 6 red radishes, trimmed and
  thinly sliced lengthwise
– juice of 1 lemon, strained
– 3½ oz/100 g mâche (corn
  salad)
– 10 black olives, pitted
– extra-virgin olive oil, for
  drizzling
– salt

Put the radishes into a salad bowl, and sprinkle with the lemon juice. Add the mâche (corn salad) and olives, drizzle with olive oil, and season with salt to taste. Mix gently and let the flavors mingle for 10 minutes before serving.

CARPACCIO DI SEDANO
ALLE ACCIUGHE
CELERIAC CARPACCIO WITH ANCHOVIES

EASY

– Preparation time: *25 minutes*
  + 30 minutes marinating
– Calories per serving: *390*
– *Serves 4*

INGREDIENTS

– 2 small celeriac, peeled and
  thinly sliced
– juice of 1 lemon, strained
– ⅔ cup (5 fl oz/150 ml) extra-
  virgin olive oil
– 2 tablespoons white wine
  vinegar
– 3 canned anchovies in oil,
  drained and chopped
– 1 tablespoon capers, drained,
  rinsed, and chopped
– 1 bunch arugula (rocket),
  leaves separated
– 2 oz/50 g Parmesan cheese,
  shaved
– salt and pepper

Put the celeriac into a bowl. Combine the lemon juice
and 4 tablespoons of the oil, then pour the mixture over
the celeriac, cover with plastic wrap (clingfilm) and
marinate for 30 minutes.

Combine the remaining oil and the vinegar in a bowl,
season with salt and pepper, and add the anchovies and
capers. Arrange a bed of arugula (rocket) on 4 serving
plates, put slices of celeriac on top, drizzle the dressing
over them, and top with the shaved Parmesan.

INSALATA DI TOPINAMBUR CON CARCIOFI
JERUSALEM ARTICHOKE SALAD

EASY

– Preparation time: *25 minutes*
– Calories per serving: *281*
– *Serves 4*

INGREDIENTS

– 14 oz/400 g Jerusalem artichokes, peeled and thinly sliced
– 4 globe artichoke hearts
– juice of 1 lemon, strained
– 1 carrot, cut into thin sticks
– 4 tablespoons extra-virgin olive oil
– salt and pepper

Put the Jerusalem artichokes into a salad bowl. Thinly slice the artichoke hearts, sprinkle with a little of the lemon juice, and add to the bowl. Add the carrot. Beat together the oil and 2 tablespoons of the remaining lemon juice in a bowl and season with salt and pepper. Pour the dressing over the salad, mix gently, and serve.

CICORIA E CRESCIONE ALL'ARANCIA

BELGIAN ENDIVE AND WATERCRESS WITH ORANGE

EASY

– Preparation time: *25 minutes*
– Calories per serving:
  229–153
– *Serves 4–6*

INGREDIENTS

– 2 heads Belgian endive
  (chicory)
– 1 orange
– 1 green apple
– 1 bunch watercress, cut into
  sprigs
– 4 tablespoons extra-virgin
  olive oil
– 1 tablespoon walnut oil
– juice of ½ lemon, strained
– pepper

Separate the Belgian endive (chicory) into leaves. Peel the orange, removing all traces of the bitter white pith, and cut into segments between the membranes. Peel and core the apple, cut into circles, and then cut these in half. Arrange the endive, orange segments, apple slices, and watercress sprigs decoratively on a serving platter.

Whisk the olive oil, walnut oil, lemon juice, and a pinch of pepper together in a bowl. Drizzle the dressing over the salad, rest for 5 minutes, and then serve.

INSALATA DI RADICCHIO E FINOCCHIO

RADICCHIO AND FENNEL SALAD

EASY

– Preparation time: *15 minutes*
– Calories per serving: *127–85*
– *Serves 4*

INGREDIENTS

– 1 bulb fennel, cut into
  quarters
– 1 large head radicchio
– red wine vinegar, for
  drizzling
– olive oil, for drizzling
– salt

Thinly slice the fennel, preferably with a mandoline, and put into a salad bowl. Cut the radicchio into thin strips and add to the fennel. Season with salt, drizzle with vinegar and oil to taste, toss lightly, and serve.

OVETTI NEL NIDO
QUAIL EGGS AND ASPARAGUS

AVERAGE

– Preparation time: *20 minutes*
– Cooking time: *10 minutes*
– Calories per serving: *210*
– *Serves 8*

INGREDIENTS

– 1 soft-boiled egg
– ⅔ cup (5 fl oz/150 ml)
  extra-virgin olive oil
– 10 green olives, pitted
  (optional)
– 1 tablespoon white wine
– 1 tablespoon white wine
  vinegar
– 1 tablespoon chopped
  fresh parsley
– 1 tablespoon chopped
  fresh marjoram
– 2¼ lb/1 kg asparagus,
  trimmed
– 16 quail eggs
– 1 lettuce heart, shredded
– salt and pepper

Shell the soft-boiled egg, then halve and scoop out the yolk into a bowl. Add the olive oil, olives if using, wine, and vinegar, season with salt and pepper, pour in 3 tablespoons water, and whisk with a fork until thoroughly combined. Sprinkle with the parsley and marjoram and set the sauce aside.

Trim the asparagus spears to the same length and tie in a bundle with kitchen (twine) string. Bring a tall saucepan of lightly salted water to a boil. Add the asparagus, standing it upright with the tips protruding above the water level. Cover and simmer for 4–5 minutes, or until tender. Lift out the asparagus and drain on paper towels. Let cool.

Put the quail eggs into a saucepan of cold water, bring to a boil, and boil for 3½ minutes. Remove from the heat, drain off the hot water, cover with cold water, and cool. When cold, carefully shell and cut them in half. Make a bed of shredded lettuce in the center of a serving plate.

Put the halved quail eggs on top. Slice the asparagus spears lengthwise and arrange them around the sides to resemble a nest. Pour the sauce over the salad and serve immediately.

STEAMED
BOILED
STEWED

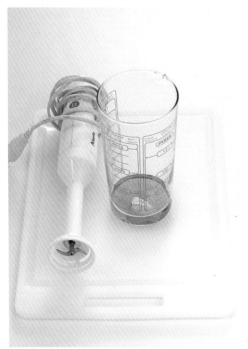

TECHNIQUE

VERDURE AL VAPORE
STEAMED VEGETABLES

EASY

– Preparation time: *10 minutes*
– Cooking time: *5–10 minutes*
– Calories per serving: *480*
– *Serves 4*

INGREDIENTS

– 1 lb 450 g pumpkin or squash
– 1 head cauliflower
– 1 head broccoli
– 4 potatoes
– ⅓ cup (3½ oz/ 100 g) yogurt
– scant ½ cup (3½ fl oz/ 100 ml) extra-virgin olive oil
– 1 small bunch chives
– 1 tablespoon balsamic vinegar
– 1 teaspoon mild mustard
– salt

STEP 1
Cut the peeled pumpkin into ¾–1 inch/2–3 cm cubes, cut and separate the cauliflower and the broccoli into florets, rinse under cold water, and drain. Peel the potatoes, rinse, and cut them into segments.

STEP 2
Place the potatoes and pumpkin in the steamer basket and cook them for 5–6 minutes. Add the cauliflower and broccoli and continue steaming for another 10 minutes.

STEP 3
To make the dressing, mix the yogurt with 3 tablespoons of oil, a pinch of salt, and 1 tablespoon of coarsely chopped chives. Pour 4 tablespoons of oil into a bowl, add the vinegar, mustard, and a pinch of salt and whisk with an immersion stick until the sauce is very well blended and smooth.

STEP 4
When the vegetables are ready, arrange them on a serving dish, handing around the vinaigrette and yogurt sauce separately.

ASPARAGI AL BURRO PROFUMATO DI LIMONE
ASPARAGUS IN LEMON BUTTER

EASY

– Preparation time: *30 minutes*
– Cooking time: *10 minutes*
– Calories per serving: *196*
– *Serves 4*

INGREDIENTS

– 2¼ lb/1 kg asparagus, trimmed
– 6 tablespoons (3 oz/80 g) butter
– juice of ½ lemon, strained
– salt and black pepper

Trim the asparagus spears to the same length. and tie in a bundle with kitchen twine (string). Bring a tall saucepan of lightly salted water to a boil. Add the asparagus, standing it upright with the tips protruding above the water level. Cover and simmer for 6–8 minutes, or until tender. Lift out the asparagus and drain on paper towels, then cut the twine and put the spears on a serving plate. Season lightly with salt.

Melt the butter in a heatproof bowl set over a saucepan of barely simmering water. Stir in the lemon juice, then remove from the heat and pour the flavored butter carefully over the asparagus. Season with black pepper and serve immediately.

FRITEDDA

ARTICHOKE, FAVA BEAN, AND PEA SALAD

– Preparation time: *30 minutes*
– Cooking time: *40 minutes*
– Calories per serving: *980*
– *Serves 8*

INGREDIENTS

– juice of 1 lemon, strained
– 8 globe artichokes
– scant ½ cup (3½ fl oz/
  100 ml) olive oil
– 1 large onion, thinly sliced
– 3¼ lb/1.5 kg fava (broad)
  beans, shelled (3¼ cups
  prepared)
– 3¼ lb/1.5 kg peas, shelled
  (3¼ cups prepared)
– 3 tablespoons white wine
  vinegar
– 1 teaspoon sugar
– salt and pepper

Fill a bowl halfway with water and stir in the lemon juice. Trim the artichoke stems (stalks), remove any coarse leaves and the chokes, and cut the artichokes into wedges, adding them immediately to the acidulated water to prevent discoloration.

Heat 2 tablespoons of the oil in a large saucepan, add the onion, and cook over low heat, stirring occasionally, for 5 minutes, until softened and translucent. Drain the artichokes, add to the pan, and cook, stirring occasionally, for a few minutes, then stir in the fava (broad) beans. Drizzle with a little hot water and simmer for 20 minutes. Stir in the peas and simmer for another 10 minutes or until tender (depending on size).

Mix the vinegar and sugar together in a bowl. Season the vegetables with salt and pepper, sprinkle with the vinegar mixture, increase the heat to high, and cook until evaporated. Transfer to a serving plate and cool completely before serving.

CAVOLINI DI BRUXELLES ALLA PARMIGIANA
PARMESAN BRUSSELS SPROUTS

EASY

– Preparation time: *15 minutes*
– Cooking time: *20 minutes*
– Calories per serving: *183*
– *Serves 4*

INGREDIENTS

– 1¾ lb/800 g Brussels sprouts, trimmed
– 2 tablespoons (1 oz/25 g) butter
– pinch of freshly grated nutmeg
– generous ¾ cup (2¼ oz/ 65 g) grated Parmesan cheese
– salt and pepper

Bring a large saucepan of water to a boil, add the Brussels sprouts, and cook for 15 minutes, then drain.

Melt the butter in another saucepan and, when golden brown, add the Brussels sprouts and cook over low heat for a few minutes. Season with salt and pepper and add the nutmeg. Transfer to a warm serving dish, sprinkle with the grated Parmesan cheese, and serve.

CREMA DI ASPARAGI
CREAM OF ASPARAGUS SOUP

EASY

– Preparation time: *10 minutes*
– Cooking time: *45 minutes*
– Calories per serving: *243*
– *Serves 4*

INGREDIENTS

– 1 lb 5 oz/600 g green
  asparagus, spears trimmed
– 4 tablespoons (2 oz/50 g)
  butter
– 1 onion, thinly sliced
– 2 tablespoons all-purpose
  (plain) flour
– scant ½ cup (3½ fl oz/
  100 ml) white wine
– 4 cups (32 fl oz/950 ml)
  vegetable broth (stock)
– 2–3 tablespoons heavy
  (double) cream
– salt and pepper

Cut off and reserve the asparagus tops and chop the stems (stalks). Melt the butter in a large saucepan, add the onion, and cook over low heat, stirring occasionally, for 5 minutes, until softened. Add the asparagus stems and cook for a few minutes, then sprinkle with the flour, stir well, and pour in the wine and broth (stock). Season with salt and pepper and cook over low heat, stirring frequently, for 30 minutes.

Transfer the mixture to a food processor and process to a puree. Bring 1½ cups (12 fl oz/350 ml) water to a boil in a saucepan, add the asparagus spears, and boil for 2 minutes. Pour the puree into a clean pan and reheat until hot. Drain the asparagus spears and add to the soup with the cream. Serve in soup bowls.

CIPOLLINE ALLA SALVIA
PEARL ONIONS WITH SAGE

EASY

– Preparation time: *10 minutes*
– Cooking time: *45 minutes*
– Calories per serving: *160*
– *Serves 4*

INGREDIENTS

– 1 tablespoon olive oil
– 2 oz/50 g pancetta, chopped
– 1 lb 2 oz/500 g pearl (baby) onions
– 5 fresh sage leaves
– salt

Heat the oil in a saucepan, add the pancetta, and cook over high heat, stirring occasionally, for 5 minutes. Add the onions and sage, season with salt, and cook over high heat until lightly browned all over. Reduce the heat, add 5 tablespoons water, and cook, covered, over low heat for about 30 minutes.

CIMETTE DI CAVOLFIORE
AL GORGONZOLA
CAULIFLOWER FLORETS WITH GORGONZOLA CHEESE

EASY

– Preparation time: *10 minutes*
– Cooking time: *10 minutes*
– Calories per serving: *308*
– *Serves 4*

INGREDIENTS

– 1 head cauliflower, separated into florets
– 1½ cups (7 oz/200 g) chopped Gorgonzola piccante cheese or any mild blue cheese
– ½ cup (4 fl oz/120 ml) milk
– 2 tablespoons (1 oz/30 g) butter, at room temperature
– 1 tablespoon brandy
– 1 teaspoon cumin seeds
– salt and pepper

Steam the cauliflower florets in a steamer for 10 minutes until al dente (tender but still firm to the bite).

Meanwhile, put the chopped cheese, milk, softened butter, and brandy into a blender or food processor, season with salt and pepper, and process until smooth. Drain the cauliflower florets, arrange them in a fairly deep serving dish, and pour the Gorgonzola cheese sauce over them. Sprinkle with cumin seeds and serve.

Tip: If you do not like the strong taste of cumin seeds, you can replace them with a generous grinding of black pepper or with ¼ cup (1 oz/30 g) of chopped, toasted hazelnuts.

GNOCCHI DI PATATE E SPINACI
POTATO AND SPINACH GNOCCHI

AVERAGE

– Preparation: *50 minutes*
– Cooking: *10 minutes*
– Calories per serving: *526*
– *Serves 4*

INGREDIENTS

– 1½ lb/700 g spinach
– 7 floury potatoes (1¾ lb/
  800 g), peeled and quartered
– 1¾ cups (7½ oz/210 g) all-
  purpose (plain) flour, plus
  extra for dusting
– 2 egg yolks, lightly beaten
– 4 tablespoons (2 oz/50 g)
  butter, melted
– ⅔ cup (2 oz/50 g) freshly
  grated Parmesan cheese
– salt

Wash the spinach. In a deep saucepan, cook the spinach for 5 minutes, covered, so that the spinach wilts down, stirring every now and again to make sure it cooks evenly. Drain, squeezing out as much liquid as possible, and chop finely.

Put the potatoes into a large saucepan of lightly salted cold water and bring to a boil. Cook the potatoes for 20–25 minutes, or until tender, then drain, return to the pan, and mash while still hot. Add the spinach and flour to the potatoes and mix together. Season with salt, beat in the egg yolks, and knead the dough for a few minutes (overkneading leads to a chewy texture).

Divide dough into quarters and shape one at a time into cylinder, about 12 inches/30 cm long and 1¼ inches/3 cm wide. Cut into 12 and then shape each piece into a ball using your hands. Dust lightly with flour.

Bring a large saucepan of lightly salted water to a boil, add the gnocchi, in batches, and remove with a slotted spoon as they rise to the surface. Drain well and arrange in a warm serving dish. Pour the butter over them and sprinkle with the Parmesan cheese. Serve.

CAVOLI AL LARDO AFFUMICATO
CABBAGE WITH SMOKED BACON

EASY

– Preparation time: *30 minutes*
– Cooking time: *45 minutes*
– Calories per serving: *237*
– *Serves 6*

INGREDIENTS

– 3 tablespoons oil
– 1 onion, chopped
– 1 clove garlic
– 2 oz/50 g lardo or smoked bacon, diced
– 1 large head cabbage, ribs removed and leaves sliced
– ½ cup (4 fl oz/120 ml) dry white wine
– 2 bay leaves
– salt and pepper

Heat the oil in a Dutch oven (casserole) over medium-heat, add the onion, garlic clove, and bacon, and cook until the onion is translucent. Remove and discard the garlic, add the cabbage, and cook for 2 minutes. Add the wine and cook until it has evaporated. Check the seasoning for salt and pepper.

Add the bay leaves, pour in ½ cup (4 fl oz/120 ml) hot water to cover the cabbage, and cook for 40 minutes, or until the water has been completely absorbed. Remove from the heat, transfer the cabbage to a serving dish, and serve, keeping the bay leaves only for decoration.

Tip: When cabbage is cooked, the sulfur that it contains actually doubles. To minimize the odor, roll a piece of bread into a small ball, then dip it into vinegar and add to the boiling water.

Note: Traditionally, Italians make this dish with lardo, which is cured fat without meat. This dish is just as delicious with smoked bacon.

STEAMED, BOILED, STEWED

PORRI AL POMODORO
LEEKS AND TOMATOES

EASY

– Preparation time: *20 minutes*
– Cooking time: *40 minutes*
– Calories per serving: *220*
– *Serves 4*

INGREDIENTS

– 3 tablespoons olive oil
– 1 shallot, finely chopped
– 4 tomatoes, peeled, seeded, and coarsely chopped
– 1 clove garlic, finely chopped
– 1 sprig fresh thyme, chopped
– ½ cup (4 fl oz/120 ml) dry white wine
– 4 leeks, thinly sliced
– salt and pepper

Pour the oil into a large saucepan, add a scant ½ cup (3½ oz/100 ml) water, and heat gently. Add the shallot and cook over low heat, stirring occasionally, for 5 minutes, until softened. Add the tomatoes, garlic, and thyme, and season with salt and pepper. Increase the heat to medium-high, pour in the wine, and cook until the alcohol has evaporated. Reduce the heat and simmer for 15 minutes.

Meanwhile, bring another saucepan of salted water to a boil, add the leeks, and blanch for 2–3 minutes, then drain well. Stir the leeks into the tomato mixture, and simmer, covered, for another 15 minutes. Uncover and let any remaining liquid evaporate. Transfer the vegetables to a warm serving dish and serve.

CICORIA AL PEPERONCINO
BELGIAN ENDIVE WITH CHILE

EASY

– Preparation time: *10 minutes*
– Cooking time: *25 minutes*
– Calories per serving: *138*
– *Serves 4*

INGREDIENTS

– 8 heads Belgian endive (chicory)
– 3 tablespoons olive oil
– 3 cloves garlic
– 1 fresh red chile, seeded and chopped
– salt and pepper

Bring a large saucepan of salted water to a boil, add the endive (chicory), and cook for 15 minutes, then drain, and squeeze out the excess liquid.

Heat the oil in a skillet or frying pan, add the garlic and chile, and cook over low heat for 1 minute, or until the garlic is lightly browned. Add the endive to the skillet, season with salt and pepper, and cook for another 10 minutes. Remove and discard the garlic.

Remove from the heat and serve.

ZUPPA DI CAVOLO NERO
CAVOLO NERO SOUP

EASY

– Preparation time: *15 minutes*
– Cooking time: *35 minutes*
– Calories per serving: *229*
– *Serves 6*

INGREDIENTS

– 3 tablespoons olive oil
– 1 onion, finely chopped
– 2 cavolo nero, shredded
– 6¼ cups (50 fl oz/1.5 liters) vegetable broth (stock)
– 9 slices bread
– 1 clove garlic, halved
– salt and pepper

Heat the oil in a large saucepan or ovenproof Dutch oven (casserole), add the onion, and cook over low heat, stirring occasionally, for 5 minutes until softened. Increase the heat to medium-high, add the cavolo nero, pour in the broth (stock), and season with salt and pepper. Bring to a boil, then reduce the heat and simmer for 30 minutes, or until the cabbage is tender.

Meanwhile, toast the bread slices on both sides, and, while they are still warm, rub the garlic clove over them. Cut them in half and place the slices of toast in 6 individual soup bowls, ladle the soup over them, and serve immediately.

FINOCCHI SALSATI
FENNEL IN SAUCE

– Preparation time: *25 minutes*
– Cooking time: *30 minutes*
– Calories per serving: *160*
– *Serves 4*

INGREDIENTS

– 4 bulbs fennel
– generous 2 cups (17 fl oz/ 500 ml) vegetable broth (stock)
– 4 tablespoons mayonnaise
– ¾ teaspoon ketchup
– 3 drops Tabasco sauce
– 4 tablespoons orange juice
– 2 tablespoons lemon juice
– 1 sprig dill, chopped, to garnish

Discard the tough outer leaves of the fennel bulbs, cut in half from top to bottom, put into a heavy saucepan, and pour in the broth (stock). Bring to a boil over high heat, then reduce the heat and cook for about 30 minutes. Drain the fennel.

Put the mayonnaise into a bowl, add the ketchup and Tabasco sauce, and stir together until mixed. Add the orange and lemon juices to the mayonnaise mixture, a little at a time to prevent the mayonnaise from becoming too runny.

Arrange the fennel in a serving dish and spoon the mayonnaise over it, then serve. Garnish with the dill.

Tip: Instead of cooking the fennel in broth (stock) and then draining it, prepare the raw bulbs as indicated above and steam them for about 20 minutes. Cool, season lightly with salt, and dress as instructed.

ZUCCA AL ROSMARINO
PUMPKIN WITH ROSEMARY

EASY

– Preparation: *15 minutes*
– Cooking: *40 minutes*
– Calories per serving: *197*
– *Serves 4*

INGREDIENTS

– 2 tablespoons olive oil
– 2 cloves garlic
– ½ pumpkin (about 2½ lb/
  1.2 kg), peeled, seeded, and
  thinly sliced
– ¾ cup (6 fl oz/175 ml) dry
  white wine
– 1½ teaspoons finely chopped
  fresh rosemary
– salt and pepper

Heat the oil in a saucepan, add the garlic and pumpkin, and cook over medium heat, stirring occasionally, until the garlic starts to brown, then remove and discard it. Pour in the wine and cook until it has evaporated, then lower the heat and simmer until tender. Season with salt and pepper to taste and sprinkle with the rosemary. Cook for another 2–3 minutes, then serve.

GUAZZETTO DI FAGIOLI E CARCIOFI
LIMA BEAN AND ARTICHOKE STEW

– Preparation time: *40 minutes*
– Cooking time: *15 minutes*
– Calories per serving: *186*
– *Serves 4*

INGREDIENTS

– 1 small celery heart,
  separated
– 2 ripe tomatoes, skinned,
  seeded, and chopped
– 1 scallion (spring onion),
  coarsely chopped
– 3 tablespoons olive oil, plus
  extra for drizzling
– juice of 1 lemon, strained
– 2 globe artichokes or 8½ oz/
  240 g jarred artichoke hearts
– 1 clove garlic
– 1 sprig fresh parsley,
  chopped
– 1⅓ cups (9 oz/240 g)
  canned lima (butter) beans,
  drained and rinsed
– salt and pepper

Bring a saucepan of water to a boil, add the celery, and blanch for 2 minutes, or until tender, then remove with a slotted spoon and plunge into a bowl of iced water to stop cooking. Cut the celery into slices.

Put the tomatoes, scallion (spring onion), celery, and 1 tablespoon oil into a blender or food processor, season with salt and pepper, and process until thoroughly combined. Add 1 tablespoon of oil to a small saucepan, pour in the mixture, and simmer over low heat, stirring occasionally, for 10 minutes. Keep the sauce warm.

Meanwhile, if using fresh artichokes, fill a bowl halfway with water and stir in the lemon juice. Trim the artichoke stems (stalks), remove any coarse leaves and the chokes, and cut off ½ inch/1 cm from the tips of the remaining leaves, adding the artichokes immediately to the acidulated water to prevent discoloration.

Heat the oil in a saucepan, add the garlic clove, and cook over low heat, stirring occasionally, for 1 minute or until lightly browned, then remove and discard it. Drain the artichokes, cut them in half, then add to the pan with the parsley, season with salt and pepper, and sprinkle with 1 tablespoon water. Simmer for 10 minutes, then stir in the beans and heat through.

To serve, spoon 2 tablespoons of the tomato sauce onto each of 6 individual plates and top with the beans and artichokes. Drizzle with a little oil and serve.

LINGUINE AL PESTO DI ZUCCHINE, MANDORLE E MENTA

LINGUINE WITH ZUCCHINI, ALMOND, AND MINT PESTO

AVERAGE

– Preparation time: *20 minutes*
– Cooking time: *8–10 minutes*
– Calories per serving: *660*
– *Serves 6*

INGREDIENTS

– 3 tablespoons olive oil
– scant ⅓ cup (1½ oz/40 g) almond halves
– 1 lb 2 oz/500 g zucchini (courgettes), halved and seeds scooped out
– 25 fresh mint leaves
– 2 cloves garlic
– 2 tablespoons chopped fresh parsley
– ⅓ cup (2 oz/50 g) blanched almonds, chopped
– 1¼ cups (3½ oz/100 g) Parmesan cheese, grated
– ⅔ cup (5 fl oz/150 ml) olive oil, plus extra for drizzling
– 1 lb 2 oz/500 g linguine
– salt and pepper

Heat the oil in a small saucepan, add the almonds, and cook, stirring frequently, for a few minutes until browned. Remove from the heat and transfer to paper towels.

Bring a medium saucepan of salted water to a boil, add the zucchini (courgettes) and simmer over low heat for 5 minutes, until al dente (tender but still with a bite). Remove with a slotted spoon, reserving the cooking water, and let cool for 15 minutes. Put the zucchini, mint leaves, garlic, parsley, chopped almonds, and Parmesan into a food processor and process until thoroughly combined. With the motor running, gradually add the oil through the feeder tube, then season with salt and pepper. Set aside.

Bring the reserved cooking water to a boil in a large saucepan, add the linguine, bring back to a boil, and cook for 8–10 minutes, until tender but still al dente. Drain and transfer to a warm serving dish. Spoon the zucchini pesto over the pasta, drizzle with olive oil, season with pepper, and toss lightly. Garnish with the almond halves and serve immediately.

CARCIOFI AL PECORINO
ARTICHOKES WITH ROMANO

EASY

– Preparation time: *20 minutes*
  + 10 minutes soaking
– Cooking time: *35 minutes*
– Calories per serving: *369*
– *Serves 4*

INGREDIENTS

– juice of ½ lemon, strained
– 8 globe artichokes
– 3 tablespoons olive oil
– 2 garlic cloves
– 1 sprig fresh flat-leaf parsley,
  chopped
– 3½ oz/100 g romano cheese,
  shaved
– generous 1 cup (2 oz/50 g)
  fresh bread crumbs
– salt

Fill a bowl halfway with water and stir in the lemon juice. Trim the artichoke stems (stalks), remove any coarse leaves and the chokes, and cut the artichokes into wedges, adding them immediately to the acidulated water to prevent discoloration. Soak for 10 minutes.

Heat the oil in a large saucepan, add the garlic, and cook over low heat for 1 minute, or until it is lightly browned, then remove and discard the garlic. Drain the artichokes and add to the pan, season with salt, cover, and cook over low heat for 30 minutes. If necessary, add a little hot water. Arrange the artichokes in a warm serving bowl and sprinkle with the parsley, shaved romano, and bread crumbs. Mix well and serve.

GNOCCHI DI RICOTTA CON PESTO DI ZUCCHINE

RICOTTA GNOCCHI WITH ZUCCHINI PESTO

ADVANCED

– Preparation time: *30 minutes + 8 hours chilling*
– Cooking time: *2 hours 10 minutes*
– Calories per serving: *510*
– *Serves 4*

INGREDIENTS

– 1¾ cups (14 oz/400 g) drained goat milk ricotta cheese, strained (see Note)
– freshly grated nutmeg
– 1 cup (5 oz/150 g) semolina
– 5 tomato skins
– salt and pepper
– black truffle flakes, to serve (optional)

FOR THE PESTO

– 4 small zucchini (courgettes), peeled and sliced into ½-inch/1-cm-thick disks
– ¼ cup (1 oz/30 g) walnuts
– 1 tablespoon good-quality extra-virgin olive oil, plus extra for drizzling
– 1 small bunch fresh basil, plus extra to garnish
– salt

Beat the ricotta in a bowl, add nutmeg and salt to taste, then spoon the mixture into a pastry (piping) bag fitted with a ⅝ -inch/1.5-cm plain nozzle (tip).

Spread the semolina onto a tray. Pipe balls of the mixture onto a tray, roll each ball in the semolina to coat, cover, and chill in the refrigerator for about 8 hours.

Preheat the oven to 120°F/50°C/lowest gas mark setting. Arrange the tomato skins in an ovenproof dish and put into the oven for about 2 hours.

To make the pesto, bring a saucepan of salted water to a boil, add the zucchini (courgettes), and cook for 1½ minutes, or until just soft. Drain, cool in iced water, then drain again. Put into a blender or food processor with the walnuts, olive oil, basil, and salt and blend until creamy. Transfer the mixture to a heatproof bowl and set aside.

Bring a large saucepan of salted water to a boil. Add the ricotta gnocchi and cook over medium heat for 3–4 minutes. Drain well on paper towels.

Put the bowl of zucchini pesto over a saucepan of simmering water and heat through, then adjust seasoning and spoon it into the center of 4 bowls. Arrange the gnocchi on top and garnish with flakes of black truffle, if using, basil, and the tomato skins. Season with pepper and drizzle with oil before serving.

Note: Drain the ricotta in a fine-mesh strainer (sieve) overnight or pressed on paper towels until all excess moisture has been removed.

PAN-FRIED

STEP 1

STEP 2

STEP 3

STEP 4

TECHNIQUE

VERDURE IN PADELLA
SAUTEED VEGETABLES

EASY

– Preparation time: *5 minutes*
– Cooking time: *10 minutes*
– Calories per serving: *120*
– *Serves 4*

INGREDIENTS

– 3 large zucchini (courgettes)
– 4–5 tablespoons olive oil
– 1 clove garlic, crushed
– 1 heaping (heaped) tablespoon chopped fresh parsley
– salt

STEP 1
Trim and slice the zucchini (courgettes) into rounds, about ¼ inch/½ cm thick.

STEP 2
Heat the oil in a large saucepan, add the garlic, and cook over medium-low heat for 1 minute, or until it is lightly browned, then remove and discard it. Add the zucchini rounds and season with salt. Stir, cover, and cook for 5 minutes.

STEP 3
Increase the heat and continue cooking for another 3–4 minutes, or until the zucchini start to brown. Add the parsley.

STEP 4
Cook for another 1–2 minutes and stir. Serve immediately.

Tip: You can substitute chopped mint, marjoram, or thyme. This method can be used to cook almost any fresh vegetable: carrots, eggplant (aubergine), leeks, artichokes, etc.

CAPONATA CLASSICA
CLASSIC CAPONATA

Bring a saucepan of water to a boil over high heat, add the celery, and blanch for 2 minutes. Remove from the heat and when cool enough to handle, cut into small pieces. Set aside.

Divide the eggplants (aubergines) into two batches. Heat 2 tablespoons of the oil in a large skillet or frying pan, add the eggplants, and cook, stirring frequently, for 10 minutes, until golden brown. Carefully remove with a slotted spoon and drain on paper towels. Repeat with the second batch.

Heat 2 tablespoons of the oil in a heavy saucepan. Add the onion and cook over low heat, stirring occasionally, for 10 minutes, until golden, then stir in 3 tablespoons of the sugar and cook for another 10 minutes, until caramelized. Remove the pan from the heat.

Heat 2 tablespoons of the oil in a large skillet or frying pan, add the celery and caramelized onion and cook over low heat, stirring occasionally, for 5 minutes. Add the capers, olives, raisins, and pine nuts and cook, stirring occasionally, for a few minutes, then stir in the pureed canned tomato puree (passata), vinegar, 2 tablespoons sugar, basil, and eggplant. Simmer for 15 minutes, then season to taste with salt and add more sugar, if necessary. Remove the pan from the heat and transfer the caponata to a serving dish. Garnish with basil and olives.

CAROTE AL ROSMARINO
CARROTS WITH ROSEMARY

EASY

– Preparation time: *10 minutes*
– Cooking time: *20 minutes*
– Calories per serving: *90*
– *Serves 4*

INGREDIENTS

– 12 carrots, cut into thin
  sticks
– 1¼ cups (10 fl oz/300 ml)
  vegetable broth (stock)
– extra-virgin olive oil, for
  drizzling
– 1 teaspoon chopped fresh
  rosemary
– salt and pepper

Put the carrots and broth (stock) into a large skillet or frying pan, bring to a boil over medium heat, then reduce the heat and simmer, covered, for about 15 minutes. Remove the lid and season with salt and pepper to taste. If the mixture is too runny, continue cooking until it has reduced to the desired consistency. Drizzle with olive oil, sprinkle with the rosemary, and cook for another few minutes. Transfer to a warm serving dish and serve.

FAGIOLINI VERDI E GIALLI
GREEN AND YELLOW BEANS

EASY

– Preparation time: *10 minutes*
– Cooking time: *35 minutes*
– Calories per serving: *240*
– *Serves 4*

INGREDIENTS

– 2 tablespoons (1 oz/25 g) butter
– 2 tablespoons olive oil
– 1 onion, sliced
– 2 tomatoes, skinned, seeded, and coarsely chopped
– 14 oz/400 g green (French) beans, trimmed (about 3⅔ cups)
– 14 oz/400 g yellow beans, trimmed (about 3⅔ cups)
– 1 clove garlic, chopped
– 1 sprig fresh parsley, chopped
– scant 1 cup (7 fl oz/200 ml) dry white wine
– salt and pepper

Melt the butter with the oil in a pan, add the onion, and cook over low heat, stirring occasionally, for 5 minutes, until softened. Add the tomatoes, beans, garlic, and chopped parsley and stir well. Pour in the wine, season with salt and pepper, and simmer, covered, for 30 minutes. Serve hot or cold.

CROCCHETTE DI SPINACI
SPINACH CROQUETTES

AVERAGE

– Preparation time: *45 minutes, plus chilling*
– Cooking time: *30 minutes*
– Calories: *600*
– *Serves 6*

INGREDIENTS

– generous ⅓ cup (2 oz/50 g) golden raisins (sultanas)
– 2¼ lb/1 kg spinach
– 3 tablespoons (1½ oz/40 g) butter
– 1¼ cups (5 oz/150 g) all-purpose (plain) flour, plus extra for dusting
– generous 2 cups (17 fl oz/500 ml) milk
– pinch of freshly grated nutmeg
– 4 oz/120 g fontina cheese, thinly sliced
– ½ cup (1½ oz/40 g) freshly grated Parmesan cheese
– 3 egg yolks
– olive oil, for brushing
– 2 eggs
– 3 cups (5 oz/150 g) fresh bread crumbs
– vegetable oil, for deep-frying
– salt and pepper

Put the golden raisins (sultanas) into a bowl, add warm water to cover, and let soak.

Wash the spinach. In a deep saucepan, cook the spinach for 5 minutes, covered, so that the spinach wilts down, stirring every now and again to make sure it cooks evenly. Drain, squeezing out as much liquid as possible, and chop finely.

Melt the butter in a saucepan, stir in the flour (it will seem like a dry crumb), then gradually stir in the milk. Bring just to a boil, whisking continuously, then season generously with salt and pepper and add the nutmeg. Remove the pan from the heat, add the fontina and Parmesan, and stir until smooth and creamy. Stir in the egg yolks, one at a time.

Drain the raisins, squeeze out, and add to the mixture with the chopped spinach. Grease a 9 x 12-inch/23 x 30-cm baking dish, pour in the spinach mixture, and smooth the surface with a dampened spatula. Once cooled, chill in the refrigerator until the mixture feels firm to the touch.

Spread out a little flour in a dish, beat the eggs in another shallow dish, and spread out the bread crumbs in a third. Cut the cooled spinach mixture into squares and dip first in the flour, then in the beaten eggs and, finally, in the bread crumbs.

Heat the oil for deep-frying in a large saucepan so that it's hot enough to turn a cube of bread golden in 30 seconds. Add the spinach croquettes, cook for 2 minutes, then turn over and cook for another 2 minutes, until golden brown. Remove with a slotted spatula, drain on paper towels, and serve hot.

MACCHERONI CON FAGIOLINI
MACARONI WITH GREEN BEANS

– Preparation time: *20 minutes*
– Cooking time: *25 minutes*
– Calories per serving: *310*
– *Serves 4*

INGREDIENTS

– olive oil, for frying
– 2 onions, finely sliced
– 2 cloves garlic, finely
  chopped
– 1–2 red chiles, finely sliced
– 7 oz/200 g macaroni
– 14 oz/400 g green (French)
  beans, trimmed and halved
  (about 3⅔ cups)
– sea salt and pepper
– grated Parmesan cheese,
  to serve (optional)
– extra-virgin olive oil, to serve
  (optional)

Heat a large skillet or frying pan, add a little olive oil, then add the onions and slowly cook over low heat, stirring occasionally, for about 15 minutes, or until they are soft, sweet, and a little browned. Add the garlic and chiles and cook for another 5 minutes.

Meanwhile, bring a large saucepan of salted water to a boil, add the macaroni, and cook for 6–8 minutes until al dente (tender but still with a bite). Add the beans and cook for another 2 minutes.

Drain the macaroni, reserving 1 cup (8 fl oz/250 ml) of the cooking water. Add the macaroni and beans to the onion pan and stir well, adding a little of the reserved water to loosen the mixture and make a sauce. Season to taste.

Finish the dish with a little grated Parmesan cheese and a drizzle of extra-virgin olive oil, if desired.

OMELETTE AI PEPERONI
BELL PEPPER OMELET

EASY

– Preparation time: *20 minutes*
– Cooking time: *40 minutes*
– Calories per serving: *260*
– *Serves 4*

INGREDIENTS

– 3 tablespoons (1½ oz/40 g) butter
– 2 tablespoons olive oil
– 1 onion, chopped
– 2 small green bell peppers, halved, seeded, and cut into thick strips
– 3 tomatoes, peeled, seeded, and diced
– ⅓ cup (2 oz/50 g) diced cooked ham
– 4 eggs
– salt and pepper

Melt the butter with the oil in a skillet or frying pan, add the onion, and cook over low heat, stirring occasionally, for 10 minutes, until lightly browned. Add the bell peppers and cook for 5 minutes, then add the tomatoes and ham. Cook over medium heat for about 20 minutes.

Lightly beat the eggs in a bowl with salt and pepper. Pour the mixture over the vegetables and increase the heat so that the omelet cooks quickly. This omelet should be soft and puffy; turn out onto a warm serving dish.

PISELLI E CIPOLLINE
ALLO ZAFFERANO
PEAS AND PEARL ONIONS WITH SAFFRON

– Preparation time: *10 minutes*
– Cooking time: *40 minutes*
– Calories per serving: *260*
– *Serves 4*

INGREDIENTS

– 3 tablespoons (1½ oz/40 g) butter
– 2 tablespoons oil
– 5 oz/150 g pearl (baby) onions, halved
– 2⅓ cups (12 oz/350 g) fresh hulled (shelled) peas
– ¾ teaspoon saffron threads
– salt and pepper

Gently heat the butter with the oil in a skillet or frying pan, add the pearl (baby) onions, and cook over low heat for 5 minutes, or until the onions are translucent. Add the peas, season with salt and pepper, and cook for another 10 minutes.

Put the saffron in a bowl with ½ cup (4 fl oz/120 ml) warm water, then pour over the peas and onions, cover, and simmer gently for another 20 minutes.

Tip: To peel the pearl onions, try blanching them for a few minutes in boiling water before peeling—the outermost skin will soften and detach more easily.

SPINACI ALL'AGRODOLCE
SWEET AND SOUR SPINACH

EASY

– Preparation time: *20 minutes*
– Cooking time: *15 minutes*
– Calories per serving: *178*
– *Serves 4*

INGREDIENTS

– ¼ cup (1 oz/30 g) raisins or golden raisins (sultanas)
– 1¾ lb/800 g spinach, trimmed
– 2 tablespoons oil
– 1 clove garlic, crushed
– 1 tablespoon pine nuts
– 1½ tablespoons balsamic vinegar
– 2 teaspoons granulated sugar
– 1 sprig fresh parsley, chopped
– salt and pepper

Soak the raisins or golden raisins (sultanas) in a bowl of cold water to soften, then drain, if necessary, and squeeze out any excess water. Set aside.

Meanwhile, in a saucepan, cook the spinach in 4 tablespoons of water over low-medium heat for 5 minutes or until wilted, then drain thoroughly and coarsely chop.

Heat the oil in a skillet or frying pan, add the garlic clove, and cook over low heat for 1 minute, or until it is lightly browned, then remove and discard it. Add the spinach to the pan and cook gently for 4 minutes. Add the raisins or golden raisins (sultanas), pine nuts, and vinegar, then sprinkle with the sugar. Stir and turn carefully, cooking gently for another 4 minutes. Adjust the seasoning, sprinkle with the chopped parsley, and then serve.

CIME DI RAPA AL PROSCIUTTO
BROCCOLI RABE WITH HAM

EASY

– Preparation time: *10 minutes*
– Cooking time: *15 minutes*
– Calories per serving: *210*
– *Serves 4*

INGREDIENTS

– 2¼ lb/1 kg broccoli rabe
– 2 tablespoons olive oil
– 2 cloves garlic
– ½ fresh red chile, seeded
  and chopped
– ⅔ cup (3½ oz/100 g)
  cooked, cured ham,
  cut into strips
– ½ cup (1 oz/25 g) fresh
  bread crumbs
– salt

Bring a saucepan of salted water to a boil, add the turnip greens (tops), and cook for 10 minutes, then drain well. Season, put into a serving dish, and keep warm.

Heat the oil in a skillet or frying pan, add the garlic, and cook over low heat for 1 minute, or until it is lightly browned, then remove and discard the cloves. Add the chile, ham, and bread crumbs to the pan and cook, stirring occasionally, for a few minutes. Spoon the ham mixture over the turnip greens and serve.

PURÈ DI FAVE E CICORIELLE
FAVA BEAN AND WILD CHICORY PUREE

AVERAGE

– Preparation time: *25 minutes*
  + 12 hours soaking
– Cooking time: *3 hours*
  30 minutes
– Calories per serving: *680*
– *Serves 6*

INGREDIENTS

– 6¼ cups (2¼ lb/1 kg) dried
  fava (broad) beans
– 6 lb 8 oz/3 kg wild chicory
  leaves or escarole
– 2 tablespoons extra-virgin
  olive oil, plus extra to drizzle
– 1 clove garlic
– 1 onion, chopped
– 1 celery stalk, chopped
– 2 tomatoes, skinned and
  seeded
– ½ bunch fresh parsley,
  chopped
– salt and pepper

Soak the dried beans in a bowl of water for 12 hours, then drain. Put the beans into a saucepan of water and bring to a boil. Reduce the heat and simmer, covered, for 3 hours, or until soft.

Drain the beans, push them through a strainer (sieve), discarding the skins, and reserve the puree.

Bring a saucepan of salted water to a boil, add the wild chicory, and cook for 1–2 minutes, until tender. Drain and chop coarsely. Set aside.

Heat the oil in a skillet or frying pan. When hot, add the garlic and cook over low heat for 1 minute, or until it is lightly browned, then remove and discard it. Add the wild chicory and stir.

Heat the bean puree in a saucepan, then add salt to taste. Stir in the onion, celery, tomatoes, and parsley and saute for about 10 minutes. Transfer to a serving dish, top with the wild chicory, stir lightly, drizzle with oil, and season with pepper.

ORECCHIETTE CON CIME DI RAPA
ORECCHIETTE WITH BROCCOLI RABE

AVERAGE

– Preparation time: *1 hour +
1 hour drying*
– Cooking time: *25 minutes*
– Calories per serving: *550*
– *Serves 6*

FOR THE PASTA

– 1¼ cups (7 oz/200 g)
semolina flour
– 3¼ cups (14 oz/400 g) "oo"
or all-purpose (plain) flour,
plus extra for dusting
– salt

FOR THE SAUCE

– 2¼ lb/1 kg broccoli rabe
– scant ½ cup (3½ fl oz/
100 ml) olive oil
– 1 small red chile, seeded and
sliced
– 2 cloves garlic, finely sliced
– 4–5 anchovy fillets
– salt and pepper
– grated Parmesan cheese,
to serve

Mix both types of flour together in a bowl. Make a well in the center, then add a pinch of salt and enough lukewarm water to form a smooth, dense dough. Put on a lightly floured work surface and cut the dough into 8 equal pieces.

Roll each piece into a cylinder about 1 inch/2.5 cm in diameter and cover with a clean cloth. Slice 1 cylinder at a time into circles about ¼ inch/5 mm thick. Put the back of a knife on the edge of a circle and push the dough toward you so that it curls around the blade.

When you have rolled all the circles in this way, stretch each of them over the end of your thumb to make the shape of a little ear. Continue until all the dough is used. Let dry for about 1 hour.

Bring a large saucepan of salted water to a boil, add the orecchiette, and cook for 2–3 minutes, until al dente (tender but still with a bite), then drain and set aside.

For the sauce, bring a saucepan of salted water to a boil, add the broccoli rabe, and blanch for 1 minute, then drain.

Heat 2 tablespoons of oil in a skillet or frying pan, add the broccoli rabe, and cook over medium heat for about 3 minutes until cooked through. Season well with salt and pepper and set aside.

Heat the remaining oil in another skillet, add half the chile, and fry over medium heat for 1–2 minutes until softened. Add the garlic and cook for another 1–2 minutes, until fragrant. Stir in the anchovies, breaking them up with the wooden spoon. Add the cooked orecchiette and broccoli rabe and stir well. Season to taste. Transfer to a serving dish and serve with grated Parmesan cheese.

FUNGHI IN SALSA AÏOLI
MUSHROOMS WITH AIOLI

EASY

– Preparation time: *30 minutes*
– Cooking time: *20 minutes*
– Calories per serving: *340*
– *Serves 4*

FOR THE MUSHROOMS

– 1½ lb/700 g white (button) mushrooms
– juice of 1 lemon, strained
– 2 tablespoons olive oil
– 1 sprig fresh tarragon, chopped
– 4 fresh chives, chopped
– 1 sprig fresh thyme, chopped
– 1 sprig fresh chervil, chopped
– 1 teaspoon fennel seeds
– salt and pepper
– 1 sprig parsley, chopped, to garnish

FOR THE AIOLI

– 2 egg yolks
– 10 cloves garlic, finely chopped
– scant ½ cup (3½ fl oz/ 100 ml) extra-virgin olive oil
– lemon juice, strained, to taste
– salt and pepper

To make the aioli, beat the egg yolks with the garlic in a bowl. Gradually add the olive oil, beating constantly with a small whisk or wooden spoon. Season with salt, pepper, and a few drops of lemon juice to taste. Set aside.

Slice the mushrooms thinly and sprinkle with the lemon juice. Bring a saucepan of water to a boil, add the mushrooms, and blanch for a few minutes, then drain.

Heat the oil in a skillet or frying pan, add the mushrooms, herbs, and fennel seeds, and cook over medium heat, stirring frequently, for 5 minutes. Reduce the heat and cook the mushrooms slowly in their own juices for 10 minutes, or until tender. Season with salt and pepper, remove from the heat, then place in a warm serving dish and scatter over the parsley. Serve with the aioli.

CARCIOFI E FINOCCHI FRITTI
ARTICHOKE AND FENNEL FRITTERS

AVERAGE

– Preparation time: *15 minutes*
– Cooking time: *10–20 minutes*
– Calories per serving: *290*
– *Serves 4*

INGREDIENTS

– 2 bulbs fennel, cut into
  wedges
– juice of ½ lemon, strained
– 4 globe artichokes
– olive oil, for deep-frying
– salt

FOR THE BATTER

– 1 egg
– 4 tablespoons milk
– scant ½ cup (2 oz/50 g)
  all-purpose (plain) flour
– salt

Bring a saucepan of salted water to a boil, add the fennel wedges, and simmer for 5 minutes, then drain.

Fill a bowl halfway with water and stir in the lemon juice. Trim the artichoke stems (stalks), remove any coarse leaves and the chokes, and cut the artichokes into wedges, adding them immediately to the acidulated water to prevent discoloration.

To make the batter, mix the egg and milk together in a bowl, then gradually beat in the flour and a pinch of salt, beating until smooth. Let stand for 5 minutes.

Heat the oil in a deep fryer or skillet to 350–375°F/ 180–190°C, or until a cube of day-old bread browns in 30 seconds. Drain the artichokes. Dip the fennel wedges into the batter, a few at a time, and drain off the excess. Add to the hot oil and deep-fry for 5–8 minutes, until golden brown. Remove with a slotted spoon and drain on paper towels. Keep warm while you cook the remaining vegetable wedges in the same way. Pile onto a serving dish, sprinkle with salt, and serve immediately.

FRITTELLE DI PATATE AI GERMOGLI DI ROSMARINO
POTATO CAKES WITH ROSEMARY

INGREDIENTS

– 7–8 potatoes, peeled and coarsely grated (about 2¼ lb/1 kg)
– 5–6 sprigs fresh rosemary, tender tips only, finely chopped, plua extra to garnish
– 6 tablespoons (3 oz/75 g) butter
– oil, for cooking
– salt

Preheat the oven to 225°F/110°C/Gas Mark ¼, then turn it off.

Put the grated potatoes into a bowl and season with a pinch of salt, then add the rosemary and stir.

Divide the mixture into 8 small mounds and dab them lightly with paper towels to dry. Make the first potato cake: melt about ¾ tablespoon of butter with a little oil in a nonstick skillet or frying pan. Put one of the little mounds of potatoes in the center, and crush with a spoon to a diameter of 4½–6 inches/12–15 cm. Cook the disk on both sides for 2–3 minutes, then dry it on paper towels, transfer to a serving dish, and keep warm in the turned-off oven. Make the 7 other potato cakes in the same way. Garnish with the rosemary and serve immediately.

ROASTED

TECHNIQUE

PATATE AL FORNO
ROAST POTATOES

EASY

– Preparation time: *10 minutes + 15 minutes cooling*
– Cooking time: *60 minutes*
– Calories per serving: *350*
– *Serves 4*

INGREDIENTS

– 1¾ lb/800 g waxy potatoes
– 4–5 tablespoons extra-virgin olive oil
– 1 clove garlic, crushed
– 1 sprig fresh rosemary (or any other herb, such as sage or oregano), leaves coarsely chopped
– salt

STEP 1
Preheat the oven to 400°F/200°C/Gas Mark 6. Put the potatoes into a large saucepan of cold water and bring to a boil. Add a pinch of salt and cook for about 10 minutes.

STEP 2
Drain the potatoes and cool completely before peeling them. Cut them into wedges.

STEP 3
Sprinkle with the oil, crushed garlic, a pinch of salt, and the rosemary leaves.

STEP 4
Transfer the potatoes to a roasting pan lined with parchment (baking) paper and roast in the oven for about 30 minutes.

PEPERONI ARROSTITI
ROAST BELL PEPPERS

Preheat the oven to 475°F/240°C/Gas Mark 9.

Cut the bell peppers in half and discard the seeds and membrane. Line a baking sheet with foil and brush with oil. Lay the peppers on it, skin side up, and cook in the oven for 20 minutes, or until the skins turn brown.

Remove from the oven but keep the oven on. Wrap the bell peppers in the foil and, as soon as they are cool enough to handle, remove the skins and cut into strips. Heat a little oil in a skillet or frying pan, lay the bell pepper strips inside, season with salt and pepper, and sprinkle with the thyme leaves.

Transfer the bell peppers to an ovenproof dish, put back into the oven and roast for another 10 minutes, or until they are just starting to caramelize. Garnish with thyme leaves and serve lukewarm or at room temperature.

Tip: Yellow and red bell peppers work the best with this style of cooking.

VERZA AL TIMO
SAVOY CABBAGE WITH THYME

– Preparation time: *10 minutes*
– Cooking time: *25 minutes*
– Calories per serving: *210*
– *Serves 4*

INGREDIENTS

– ½ cabbage, tough leaves and stems (stalks) removed, then cut into quarters
– generous 3 cups (25 fl oz/ 750 ml) hot vegetable broth (stock)
– 3 tablespoons olive oil
– 1–2 sprig fresh thyme, leaves only
– salt and pepper

Preheat the oven to 350°F/180°C/Gas Mark 4.

Arrange the cabbage quarters in a deep ovenproof dish.

Pour the broth (stock) over the cabbage, drizzle over the oil, and sprinkle the thyme leaves on top. Season with salt and pepper.

Cover the dish with foil and cook in the oven for 20 minutes, or until the cabbage is tender. Remove the foil, increase the oven temperature to 425°F/220°C/Gas Mark 7, and cook for another 5 minutes or until the tops of the cabbages begin to brown. Transfer to a serving dish and serve.

CASTAGNE ARROSTO CON CAVOLINI DI BRUXELLES

ROAST CHESTNUTS WITH BRUSSELS SPROUTS

AVERAGE

– Preparation time: *1 hour*
– Cooking time: *1 hour*
– Calories per serving: *430*
– *Serves 4*

INGREDIENTS

– 1 lb 2 oz/500 g chestnuts
– 4 tablespoons (2 oz/50 g)
  butter, plus extra for
  greasing
– 1 shallot, chopped
– 1 lb 2 oz/500 g Brussels
  sprouts, trimmed and coarse
  leaves removed
– juice of 1 lemon, strained
– pinch of freshly grated
  nutmeg
– generous ¾ cup (3½ oz/
  100 g) grated fontina cheese
– salt and pepper

Make a slit in each chestnut with a small knife. Put them into a saucepan, pour in enough water to cover, bring to a boil, reduce the heat, and simmer for 20 minutes.

Melt half the butter in another saucepan, add the shallot, and cook over low heat, stirring occasionally, for 5 minutes, until softened. Add the Brussels sprouts and lemon juice and pour in ½ cup (4 fl oz/120 ml) water. Season with salt and pepper and stir in the nutmeg. Cook, covered, for about 10 minutes.

Meanwhile, preheat the oven to 400°F/200°C/Gas Mark 6 and grease an ovenproof dish with butter.

Drain the chestnuts and rinse under cold running water. Remove and discard the shells and inner skins and put them into the prepared dish. Add the Brussels sprouts, together with some of the cooking liquid. Sprinkle with the grated cheese, dot with the remaining butter, and bake in the oven for 30 minutes. Serve immediately straight from the dish.

RAPE IN TEGLIA CON PORRI E ZUCCA

ROAST TURNIPS WITH LEEKS AND PUMPKIN

EASY

– Preparation time: *15 minutes*
– Cooking time: *45 minutes*
– Calories per serving: *170*
– *Serves 4*

INGREDIENTS

– 7 oz/200 g pumpkin, peeled, seeded, and sliced
– 1 teaspoon fresh thyme leaves
– 3 tablespoons olive oil, plus extra for drizzling
– 1–2 leeks, trimmed and sliced
– 2 large turnips, trimmed and sliced
– 2 tablespoons sesame seeds
– salt

Preheat the oven to 400°F/200°C/Gas Mark 6.

Put the pumpkin slices onto a sheet of foil, season with salt, and sprinkle with the thyme leaves. Fold over the foil to enclose the pumpkin completely, put on a baking sheet, and bake in the oven for 30 minutes.

Heat the oil in a large saucepan, add the leeks and turnips, and cook over medium heat, stirring occasionally, for 10 minutes, or until tender. Add the pumpkin and cook for another 5 minutes. Sprinkle with the sesame seeds and drizzle with olive oil, then serve.

BAKED

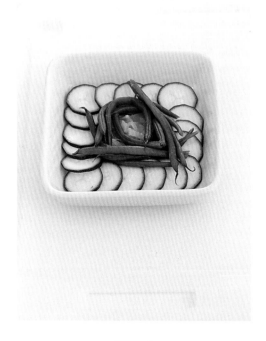

TECHNIQUE

EASY

- Preparation time: *20 minutes*
- Cooking time: *35 minutes*
- Calories per serving: *150*
- *Serves 4*

INGREDIENTS

- 2 tablespoons extra-virgin olive oil, plus extra for oiling and drizzling
- 1 shallot, cut into very thin slices
- 7 oz/200 g green (French) beans, trimmed (about 2 cups)
- 2 zucchini (courgettes), trimmed and cut into slices about ¼ inch/½ cm thick
- 2 cherry tomatoes, halved
- 2 sprigs fresh thyme, leaves only
- ⅓ cup (1 oz/25 g) grated Parmesan cheese
- salt

STEP 1

Preheat the oven to 350°F/180°C/Gas Mark 4 and lightly oil a large ovenproof dish or 4 small individual dishes. Heat the oil in a saucepan over medium heat, add the shallot and 2 tablespoons water, and cook, covered, for 5 minutes, or until translucent. In the meantime, bring a saucepan of salted water to a boil, add the beans, and cook for 5 minutes, then drain.

STEP 2

Arrange the zucchini (courgette) slices, slightly overlapping, toward the edges of each ovenproof dish, and sprinkle the shallot slices on top, followed by the beans.

STEP 3

Top with the halved cherry tomatoes. Sprinkle with a pinch of salt, the thyme leaves, and Parmesan cheese, finishing with a drizzle of oil.

STEP 4

Bake in the oven for about 30 minutes. Serve hot or cold.

PARMIGIANA DI MELANZANE
EGGPLANT PARMESAN

AVERAGE

– Preparation time: *50 minutes*
– Cooking time: *1 hour*
– Calories per serving: *480*
– *Serves 6*

INGREDIENTS

– 2¼ lb/1 kg tomatoes,
  skinned, seeded, and
  chopped
– 4 sprigs fresh basil
– pinch of sugar
– 4 eggplants (aubergines),
  sliced lengthwise, ¼ inch/
  ½ cm thick
– all-purpose (plain) flour,
  for dusting
– ⅔–¾ cups (5–6 fl oz/150–
  175 ml) olive oil, plus extra
  for drizzling
– 1¼ cups (3½ oz/100 g)
  Parmesan cheese, grated
– 9 oz/250 g mozzarella
  cheese, sliced
– 2 eggs, lightly beaten
– salt

Put the tomatoes into a heavy saucepan, tear in the basil leaves, add the sugar, and simmer gently over medium-low heat, stirring occasionally, for 30 minutes, until pulpy and thickened.

Season the eggplant (aubergine) slices with salt and dust with flour. Heat 2 tablespoons of the oil in a large skillet or frying pan, add the eggplant slices, in batches, and cook for 5 minutes on each side, until golden brown. Remove with a spatula and drain on paper towels. Cook the remaining batches in the same way, adding more oil as necessary.

Preheat the oven to 350°F/180°C/Gas Mark 4.

Spoon some of the tomato sauce over the bottom of an ovenproof dish and make a layer of eggplant slices on top. Season generously. Sprinkle with a little Parmesan, top with some slices of mozzarella, and drizzle with a little beaten egg. Continue making layers in this way until all the ingredients have been used, ending with a layer of tomato sauce. Drizzle with olive oil and bake for 30 minutes.

CAROTE AL TALEGGIO
CARROTS WITH TALEGGIO CHEESE

EASY

– Preparation time: *30 minutes*
– Cooking time: *40 minutes*
– Calories per serving: *260*
– *Serves 6*

INGREDIENTS

– butter, for greasing
– 2 tablespoons olive oil
– 1 shallot, finely chopped
– 12–14 carrots (¾ lb/800 g), cut into ½-inch/1-cm slices
– 6 oz/175 g Taleggio cheese, grated
– 2 eggs, lightly beaten
– ½ cup (1½ oz/40 g) grated Parmesan cheese
– scant ½ cup (3½ fl oz/ 100 ml) milk
– 1 tablespoon chopped fresh parsley
– salt and pepper

Preheat the oven to 325°F/170°C/Gas Mark 3 and grease an ovenproof dish with butter.

Heat the oil in a skillet or frying pan, add the shallot, and cook over low heat, stirring occasionally, for 5 minutes, until softened and translucent. Remove the shallot from the pan and set aside. Stir in the carrots and cook, stirring occasionally, for 10 minutes. Season with salt and pepper and cook for another 5 minutes, then remove from the heat.

Cut the rind from the Taleggio and discard. In a food processor, combine the Taleggio, eggs, Parmesan cheese, and milk, then season generously with salt and pepper. Put the carrots into the prepared dish, spreading them out evenly. Cover with the Taleggio cream and bake in the oven for 20 minutes. Remove from the oven, sprinkle with the chopped parsley, and serve.

PEPERONI IN TORTIERA
BELL PEPPER PIE

EASY

– Preparation time: *35 minutes*
  + 10 minutes cooling
– Cooking time: *1 hour
  20 minutes*
– Calories per serving: *168*
– *Serves 6*

INGREDIENTS

– 3 tablespoons oil, plus extra
  for greasing
– 4½ lb/2 kg red and yellow
  bell peppers
– 6 tablespoons bread crumbs
– 1 tablespoon chopped fresh
  parsley
– 1 tablespoon chopped capers
– 1 clove garlic (optional)
– salt and pepper

Preheat the oven to 350°F/180°C/Gas Mark 4 and grease a round ovenproof dish with oil.

Wrap the bell peppers in foil, put them onto a baking sheet, and cook in the oven for 1 hour. Remove from the oven and cool slightly. Halve and seed, then cut the halves into thin strips. Set aside.

Increase the oven temperature to 375°F/190°C/Gas Mark 5.

Put the bread crumbs into a bowl and mix with the chopped parsley, capers, oil, salt, and pepper. Add just enough water so that the stuffing is soft but malleable. Arrange the bell pepper strips in layers with a layer of the bread mixture between them in the prepared dish. Push the garlic clove deep into the center of the top layer, if using. Drizzle with a little oil and cook in the oven for about 20 minutes. Remove from the oven, cool, and serve.

ZUCCHINE RIPIENE
STUFFED ZUCCHINI

– Preparation time: *30 minutes*
– Cooking time: *1 hour
 10 minutes*
– Calories per serving: *890*
– *Serves 4*

INGREDIENTS

– butter, for greasing
– 6–7 zucchini (courgettes),
 halved lengthwise
– 1 small onion, finely diced
– 1 tablespoon oil
– 3½ oz/100 g lean ham, finely
 chopped
– 2 ripe tomatoes, skinned,
 seeded, and diced
– 7 oz/200 g white (button)
 mushrooms, stems (stalks)
 removed and diced
– 1 egg
– 3 tablespoons bread crumbs
– generous ⅓ cup (2 oz/50g)
 grated Grana Padano or
 Parmesan cheese
– salt and pepper
– 1 sprig parsley, chopped, to
 garnish

Preheat the oven to 350°F/180°C/Gas Mark 4 and grease an ovenproof dish with butter.

To cook the zucchini (courgettes), bring a saucepan of salted water to a boil, add them to the pan, and cook for 10 minutes, or until just tender but still firm.

Drain the zucchini, carefully scoop out some of the flesh with a spoon, put the partly hollowed-out zucchini onto a cloth, skin side up, and let dry.

Meanwhile, heat the oil in a nonstick saucepan, add the diced onion, and saute for 5 minutes, or until the onions are translucent. Add the ham and cook for 5 minutes, then add the tomatoes and bring the mixture to a gentle boil for 5 minutes, or until the sauce has thickened. Add a little water, if necessary, to loosen.

Heat a heavy saucepan, add an even layer of diced mushrooms, and cover with a lid. (Don't add any water.) Cook over high heat for 5 minutes, or until the liquid released from the mushrooms reduces completely. Add to the ham mixture, stir gently, and cook for another 5 minutes. Remove from the heat.

Lightly beat the egg in a bowl with a fork and stir into the pan, followed by the bread crumbs, grated cheese, and salt and pepper to taste. Fill the zucchini shells with the mixture, then put into the prepared ovenproof dish and cook in the oven for 30 minutes. Transfer to a serving dish to serve. Garnish with parsley.

COSTE GRATINATE CON BESCIAMELLA

BEET GREENS AU GRATIN WITH BÉCHAMEL SAUCE

EASY

– Preparation time: *20 minutes*
– Cooking time: *60 minutes*
– Calories per serving: *320*
– *Serves 4*

INGREDIENTS

– butter, plus for greasing
– 2¼ lb/1 kg beet greens
  (beetroot tops) or Swiss
  chard, white stems (cut
  in half if large) and leaves
  separated and cut into thin
  strips
– coarse salt and pepper

**FOR THE
BÉCHAMEL SAUCE**

– 3 tablespoons (1½ oz/40 g)
  butter
– scant ½ cup (1½ oz/40 g)
  all-purpose (plain) flour
– 2½ cups (20 fl oz/600 ml)
  milk
– pinch of grated nutmeg
– ½ cup (1½ oz/40 g) grated
  Parmesan cheese
– salt

Preheat the oven to 350°F/180°C/Gas Mark 4 and lightly grease an 8 x 9-inch/20 x 24-cm ovenproof dish.

Bring a large saucepan of water to a boil, add a pinch of coarse salt and the stems, and boil for about 15 minutes. Remove with a slotted spoon and set aside. Put the green leaves into the water and boil for 5 minutes, then remove with a slotted spoon.

To make the béchamel sauce, melt the butter in a saucepan, add the flour all at once, stir over low heat for 2–3 minutes, then gradually beat or stir in the milk, adding it in a constant stream. Cook the sauce for 7–8 minutes, stirring frequently.

Add a pinch of salt, the nutmeg, and pepper, then add the Parmesan cheese, stir briefly, and immediately remove from the heat. Arrange the beet stems (beetroot stalks), leaves, and the sauce in layers in the prepared ovenproof dish, ending with a topping of the sauce. Bake in the oven for about 30 minutes, then serve hot.

Tip: If you do not like béchamel sauce, mix the prepared white and green parts of the beet (beetroot) with a lightly beaten mixture of 3 eggs, 1¼ cups (10 fl oz/300 ml) of milk and ½ cup (1½ oz/40 g) grated Parmesan cheese, a pinch of salt, a little freshly ground pepper, then cook in the oven as described above.

PASTA E POMODORI AL FORNO
PASTA AND TOMATO BAKE

AVERAGE

– Preparation time: *30 minutes + 30 minutes salting*
– Cooking time: *1 hour*
– Calories per serving: *400*
– *Serves 10*

INGREDIENTS

– 4½ lb/2 kg ripe tomatoes, halved
– olive oil, for brushing and drizzling
– 1⅓ cups (3 oz/80 g) fresh bread crumbs
– ½ clove garlic, chopped
– generous ¾ cup (2½ oz/ 65 g) pecorino cheese, grated
– generous ¾ cup (2½ oz/ 65 g) Parmesan cheese, grated
– handful fresh parsley, chopped
– 1 lb 2 oz/500 g broken rigatoni or ziti pasta
– salt and pepper

FOR THE SAUCE

– scant ½ cup (3½ fl oz/ 100 ml) olive oil
– 2 cloves garlic
– 3⅓ cups (1¾ lb/800 g) canned diced or chopped tomatoes
– salt and pepper

Score the uncut surface of the halved tomatoes onto a crisscross pattern and put them on a plate, cut side up. Sprinkle with salt and let stand for 30 minutes.

Preheat the oven to 425°F/220°C/Gas Mark 7 and brush a large baking dish with oil.

Meanwhile, to make the sauce, heat the oil in a skillet or frying pan, add the garlic cloves, and cook over low heat for 1 minute, or until it is lightly browned, then remove and discard it. Add the diced tomatoes, season with salt and pepper, and cook for about 10 minutes. Season again, then set aside.

Put the bread crumbs into a bowl and mix in the chopped garlic, pecorino, Parmesan, and parsley. Pat the halved tomatoes dry with paper towels. Arrange half of them in the prepared dish and sprinkle with half the bread crumb mixture. Drizzle with oil and bake in the oven for 10 minutes, or until the top is golden brown. Remove from the oven and set aside.

Bring a large saucepan of salted water to a boil, add the pasta, and cook for 15 minutes, or until al dente (tender but firm to the bite). Drain, return the pasta to the pan, then toss in the tomato sauce and a little of the bread crumb mixture. Spread over the baked tomatoes and arrange the remaining tomatoes over the top, Sprinkle with the remaining bread crumb mixture, drizzle with oil and bake in the oven for 15 minutes, or until golden brown. Let stand for a few minutes before serving.

PORRI GRATINATI

LEEKS AU GRATIN

EASY

– Preparation time: *45 minutes*
  + 15 minutes drying
– Cooking time: *25 minutes*
– Calories per serving: *490*
– *Serves 4*

INGREDIENTS

- 2¼ lb/1 kg leeks, white parts only
- 6 tablespoons (3 oz/80 g) butter, plus extra for greasing
- ¼ cup (1 oz/30 g) all-purpose (plain) flour
- 1½ cups (12 fl oz/350 ml) milk
- 2 egg yolks
- ½ cup (2¼ oz/60 g) freshly grated Emmental cheese
- pinch of freshly grated nutmeg
- scant 1 cup (3 oz/80 g) freshly grated Parmesan cheese
- ⅓ cup (½ oz/15 g) fresh bread crumbs
- salt and pepper

Bring a large saucepan of salted water to a boil, add the leeks, and cook for about 15 minutes, then drain well, spread out on a dish towel, and let dry.

Preheat the oven to 350°F/180°C/Gas Mark 4 and grease an ovenproof dish with butter.

Melt 3 tablespoons of the butter in a large saucepan, add the leeks, and cook over low heat, turning occasionally, for a few minutes, then transfer to the prepared dish.

To make the béchamel sauce, melt the remaining butter in a saucepan, add the flour all at once, stir over low heat for 2–3 minutes, then gradually beat or stir in the milk, adding it in a constant stream. Cook the sauce for 7–8 minutes, stirring frequently.

Remove the pan from the heat, beat in the egg yolks, Emmental, and nutmeg, and season with salt and pepper. Pour the sauce over the leeks, sprinkle with the grated Parmesan cheese and bread crumbs, dot with the remaining butter, and bake for about 20 minutes, until golden brown and bubbling.

TORTA DI FRITTATE
FRITTATA CAKE

AVERAGE

– Preparation time: *30 minutes*
  + 10 minutes cooling
– Cooking time: *20 minutes*
– Calories per serving: *240*
– *Serves 6*

INGREDIENTS

– 1 small eggplant (aubergine),
  sliced
– 2 red or yellow bell peppers
– 6 eggs
– 1 sprig fresh flat-leaf parsley,
  chopped
– 1 tablespoon grated
  Parmesan cheese
– 2 tablespoons olive oil
– 2 tablespoons (1 oz/25 g)
  butter
– 3½ oz/100 g fontina cheese,
  sliced
– salt and pepper

Preheat the oven to 400°F/200°C/Gas Mark 6 and preheat the broiler (grill).

Put the eggplants (aubergines) on a broiler (grill) pan and broil for 5 minutes, or until soft and golden brown. Put the bell peppers on a nonstick baking sheet and roast in the oven for 5 minutes, or until blackened and charred, then transfer to a plastic bag and seal the top. Increase the oven temperature to 475°F/240°C/Gas Mark 9 and line a cake pan with parchment (baking) paper.

When the bell peppers are cool enough to handle, peel and seed them and cut the flesh into strips. Beat 2 eggs in one bowl and 2 eggs in another bowl, season both with salt and pepper, and divide the parsley between them. Beat the remaining eggs in a third bowl, season with salt and pepper, and stir in the grated Parmesan cheese.

Heat the oil and butter in a skillet or frying pan, pour in one bowl of the egg-and-parsley mixture, and cook for 1–2 minutes, until set on one side but still soft on the other. Slide the frittata out of the skillet and cook 2 more in the same way, with the remaining egg-and-parsley mixture and the egg-and-Parmesan mixture.

Put one of the parsley frittatas, soft side up, in the prepared pan. Cover with the eggplant and half the fontina. Put the Parmesan frittata on top of them, soft side up, and cover with the strips of bell pepper and the remaining fontina. Finally, put the second parsley frittata on top, soft side down, and bake in the oven for 10 minutes. Serve hot or cold.

TORTA DI CIPOLLE ALL'ANTICA
OLD-FASHIONED ONION TART

EASY

- Preparation time: *20 minutes + 10 minutes soaking*
- Cooking time: *1 hour 15 minutes*
- Calories per serving: *470*
- *Serves 6*

INGREDIENTS

- 4 tablespoons (2 oz/50 g) butter, plus extra for greasing
- all-purpose (plain) flour, for dusting
- 1 cup (5 oz/150 g) golden raisins (sultanas)
- 1 cup (8 fl oz/250 ml) dry white wine
- 7 oz/200 g store-bought pie dough (shortcrust pastry), thawed if frozen
- 8–9 onions (about 2¼ lb/ 1 kg) onions, thinly sliced
- marrow from 2 beef bones, diced
- pinch of sugar
- salt and pepper

Preheat the oven to 325°F/160°C/Gas Mark 3. Grease an 8-inch/20-cm tart or quiche pan with butter and sprinkle with flour, tipping the pan to coat.

Put the golden raisins (sultanas) into a bowl, pour the wine over them, and soak.

Meanwhile, roll out the pie dough (shortcrust pastry) on a lightly floured work surface and line the prepared pan, trimming the edges. Set aside the scraps. Prick the bottom all over with a fork. Line with parchment (baking) paper, fill with pie weights (baking beans), and bake blind for 15 minutes. Remove the pastry shell (case) and increase the oven temperature to 350°F/180°C/Gas Mark 4.

Meanwhile, melt the butter in a skillet or frying pan, add the onions, and cook over low heat, stirring occasionally, for 10 minutes, or until golden brown. Stir in the beef marrow, the golden raisins with the wine, and the sugar, season with salt and pepper, and cook for 20 minutes, until the wine has evaporated. Remove the weights and parchment paper from the pastry shell, pour in the onion mixture, and spread evenly. Roll out the dough scraps, cut into thin strips, brush the ends with water, and arrange in a lattice over the top of the tart. Bake in the oven for 30 minutes.

TORTA DI BIETOLINE E RICOTTA
SWISS CHARD AND RICOTTA PIE

AVERAGE

– Preparation time: *1 hour +
  30 minutes soaking*
– Cooking time: *30 minutes*
– Calories per serving: *530*
– *Serves 8*

INGREDIENTS

– 1 lb 2 oz/500 g Swiss chard
– generous 1 cup (9 oz/250 g)
  ricotta cheese
– 1 cup (3 oz/80 g) grated
  Parmesan cheese
– 1 small onion, chopped
– 1 egg, beaten
– 4 tablespoons olive oil
– salt and pepper

FOR THE PIE DOUGH
(PASTRY)

– scant 4¼ cups (1 lb 2 oz/
  500 g) all-purpose (plain)
  flour
– 6 tablespoons olive oil

Soak the Swiss chard leaves and tender stems (stalks) in a bowl of salted water for 30 minutes, then drain.

Preheat the oven to 375°F/190°C/Gas Mark 5 and line the bottom and sides of an 8 x 10-inch/20 x 25-cm baking dish with parchment (baking) paper.

To make the pie dough (pastry), put the flour into a bowl, add the oil and a scant ½ cup (3½ fl oz/100 ml) water, and mix together to form a dough. No salt is needed. Shape the dough into a fat cylinder, then cut into 4 equal pieces. Lightly flour a work surface and roll each piece of dough into a thin 8–10-inch/20–25-cm sheet. Use 2 dough sheets to cover the bottom of the prepared dish.

Pour 2 cups (16 fl oz/475 ml) salted water into a large saucepan and bring to a boil, add the Swiss chard, and cook for 2–3 minutes or until tender, turning the chard over frequently to make sure it cooks evenly. Drain and rinse under cold running water. When cool, squeeze the chard dry with your hands and chop.

In a large bowl, combine the chard, ricotta, Parmesan cheese, onion, egg, and salt and pepper and mix well. Spread the mixture in the dough-lined dish and cover with the remaining sheets of dough. Using a toothpick or fine skewer, prick the pie several times almost down to the bottom of the dough.

Sprinkle the top with the oil and 4 tablespoons water and bake in the oven for about 30 minutes, until the pie is golden brown and piping hot. Let stand for 5 minutes before serving.

TORTA DI FINOCCHI
FENNEL PIE

Preheat the oven to 350°F/180°C/Gas Mark 4 and grease a large pie dish with butter.

Melt the butter in a large saucepan, add the fennel, and cook over medium-low heat, stirring occasionally, for 8–10 minutes, until softened.

Roll out two-thirds of the dough on a lightly floured work surface and line the pie dish with the dough. Trim the edges and brush the rim with water. Spoon the fennel into the dish and top with the slices of cheese.

Beat the whole eggs and milk together in a bowl, season with salt and pepper, and pour the mixture over the fennel and cheese. Roll out the remaining dough, place it over the pie, and press the edges to seal. Brush the surface with egg yolk and bake in the oven for about 40 minutes, until golden brown.

SFORMATO DI ZUCCA
PUMPKIN TART

AVERAGE

– Preparation time: *45 minutes*
– Cooking time: *1 hour
  10 minutes*
– Calories per serving: *450*
– *Serves 4*

INGREDIENTS

– 2 tablespoons (1 oz/25 g)
  butter, plus extra for
  greasing
– 1 onion, sliced
– 2¼ lb/1 kg pumpkin, peeled,
  seeded, and diced (about
  5¾ cups prepared)
– 1 quantity Béchamel Sauce
  (see page 148)
– scant ⅔ cup (2 oz/50 g)
  Parmesan cheese, grated
– 2 egg yolks
– ⅓ cup (1½ oz/40 g) pine
  nuts
– salt and pepper

Preheat the oven to 325°F/160°C/Gas Mark 3 and grease an 8-inch/20-cm tart pan with butter.

Melt the butter in a large saucepan, add the onion, and cook over low heat, stirring occasionally, for 5 minutes, until softened. Add the pumpkin and ⅔ cup (5 fl oz/ 150 ml) water and cook, stirring and mashing occasionally, until the pumpkin turns to a soft puree.

Stir in the béchamel sauce, grated Parmesan cheese, egg yolks, and pine nuts, and season with salt and pepper. Pour the mixture into the prepared pan and bake in the oven for 1 hour.

Increase the oven temperature to 350°F/180°C/Gas Mark 4 and bake for another 10 minutes. Remove from the oven and cool completely before turning out.

PURÈ GRATINATO CON PANCETTA E TIMO
POTATO AND BACON BAKE

EASY

– Preparation time: *30 minutes*
  + 10 minutes cooling
– Cooking time: *1 hour*
  15 minutes
– Calories per serving: *530*
– *Serves 4*

INGREDIENTS

– 9 potatoes (about 2¼ lb/
  1 kg), peeled and cut into
  large pieces
– 4 tablespoons (2 oz/50 g)
  butter, plus extra for
  greasing
– 1 tablespoon olive oil
– 3½ oz/100 g bacon, cut
  crosswise into thin strips
– 1 egg, lightly beaten
– 3 oz/80 g provolone cheese,
  coarsely grated
– 3 sprigs fresh thyme, finely
  chopped
– 4 tablespoons fresh bread
  crumbs
– salt and pepper

Put the potatoes into a steaming basket. Bring 2-inches/ 5-cm water to a boil in a saucepan. Insert the steamer, cover, and cook for 20–30 minutes, until tender. Transfer the potatoes to a bowl and crush with a fork, then cool slightly. Set aside.

Preheat the oven to 400°F/200°C/Gas Mark 6 and grease an ovenproof dish with butter.

Heat the oil in a skillet or frying pan, add the bacon strips, and cook over medium heat, turning occasionally, for 6–8 minutes, until slightly crisp. Mix the crushed potatoes with the egg and cheese, and season with salt and pepper. Add the bacon and thyme, then spoon the potato mixture into the prepared dish, sprinkle with the bread crumbs, and dot with the butter. Bake in the oven for 30 minutes, until golden brown and crunchy on top. Serve immediately.

TORTA SALATA CON SPINACI, RICOTTA E FETA

SPINACH QUICHE WITH SALTED CHEESE AND FETA

AVERAGE

– Preparation time: *15 minutes*
– Cooking time: *30–40 minutes*
– Calories per serving: *410*
– *Serves 6*

INGREDIENTS

– 9 oz/250 g store-bought puff pastry dough, thawed if frozen
– all-purpose (plain) flour, for dusting
– 4 cups (7 oz/200 g) spinach, chopped
– 4 eggs
– scant 1 cup (7 oz/200 g) ricotta salata or salted soft cheese, crumbled
– 3½ oz/100 g feta cheese, drained and diced
– 4 tablespoons pine nuts, toasted
– olive oil, for drizzling
– salt and pepper

Preheat the oven to 400°F/200°C/Gas Mark 6. Place a baking sheet in the center of the oven to heat.

Roll out the dough on a lightly floured work surface and use to line an 8-inch/20-cm tart pan. Prick all over with a fork. Place in the refrigerator to chill.

Heat a large saucepan over medium heat and add the spinach. Using two wooden spoons to turn it over, cook until wilted. Place in a strainer (sieve) to drain and cool. Squeeze the spinach until it is dry, then chop coarsely.

Beat the eggs and ricotta together in a bowl, then stir in the spinach and feta. Season with pepper and lightly with salt, and pour the mixture into the pastry shell (case). Sprinkle with the pine nuts and drizzle with oil.

Put the pan on a hot baking sheet and bake in the oven for 10 minutes, then reduce the oven temperature to 350°F/180°C/Gas Mark 4 and bake for another 20–30 minutes until set. Remove the pan from the oven and serve the quiche lukewarm.

INVOLTINI DI CAVOLO ALLA RICOTTA
RICOTTA AND SAVOY CABBAGE ROLLS

EASY

– Preparation time: *20 minutes*
– Cooking time: *20 minutes*
– Calories per serving: *340*
– *Serves 4*

INGREDIENTS

– 8 savoy cabbage leaves
– 11 oz/300 g Swiss chard, leaves only
– scant 1 cup (7 oz/225 g) ricotta cheese
– ¼ cup (¾ oz/20 g) grated Parmesan cheese
– 2 eggs, lightly beaten
– 2 cups (1 lb 2 oz/500 g) tomato sauce
– salt and pepper

Preheat the oven to 350°F/180°C/Gas Mark 4.

Bring a large saucepan of salted water to a boil, add the cabbage leaves, and blanch for 5 minutes, then drain and plunge into a bowl of iced water. Drain again and spread out on a dish towel.

Bring another saucepan of salted water to a boil, add the Swiss chard, and cook for 10–15 minutes, then drain, squeezing out as much liquid as possible. Chop finely, put into a bowl, and stir in the ricotta, Parmesan cheese, and eggs. Season with salt and pepper and mix well.

Divide the mixture among the cabbage leaves. Roll up each leaf and tie with kitchen twine (string). Place the cabbage rolls in an ovenproof Dutch oven (casserole), pour in the tomato sauce, cover, and bake for about 1 hour. Serve.

TORTA ALLA RUCOLA E TALEGGIO
ARUGULA AND TALEGGIO PIE

AVERAGE

– Preparation time: *15 minutes*
+ 1 hour resting
– Cooking time: *50 minutes*
– Calories per serving: *630*
– *Serves 6*

INGREDIENTS

– 1⅔ cups (7 oz/200 g) all-purpose (plain) flour, plus extra for dusting
– 1 tablespoon poppy seeds
– 1 tablespoon chopped fresh marjoram
– 7 tablespoons (3½ oz/100 g) butter, chilled and diced, plus extra for greasing
– salt

FOR THE FILLING

– 10 cups (7 oz/200 g) arugula (rocket)
– 1⅔ cups (11 oz/300 g) cream cheese
– 7 oz/200 g Taleggio cheese, diced
– 2 tablespoons bread crumbs
– 2 eggs
– salt and pepper

Sift the flour with a pinch of salt into a mound on a work surface, sprinkle with the poppy seeds and marjoram, add the butter, and rub it in with your fingertips. Add enough cold water to make a soft dough, then shape into a ball, cover with plastic wrap (clingfilm), and rest for 1 hour.

Preheat the oven to 350°F/180°C/Gas Mark 4 and grease an 8-inch/20-cm tart or quiche pan with butter.

Bring a saucepan of salted water to a boil, add the arugula (rocket), and cook for a few minutes, then drain, squeezing out as much liquid as possible. Put the arugula into a food processor with both cheeses, the bread crumbs, and eggs and process at low speed, then season with salt and pepper.

Roll out the dough on a lightly floured work surface, and use to line the prepared pan. Trim the edges and reserve the scraps. Fill the pastry shell (case) with the arugula-and-cheese mixture. Roll out the dough scraps, cut into thin strips, brush the ends with water, and arrange in a lattice over the top of the pie. Bake in the oven for about 40 minutes.

SOUFFLÈ DI FAGIOLINI
GREEN BEAN SOUFFLE

INGREDIENTS

– butter, for greasing
– 1¾ lb/800 g green (French)
  beans, trimmed
– 2 tablespoons freshly grated
  Parmesan cheese
– 4 eggs, separated

FOR THE
BÉCHAMEL SAUCE

– 6 tablespoons butter
– ⅔ cup (3 oz/80 g)
  all-purpose (plain) flour
– generous 2 cups (17 fl oz/
  500 ml) milk
– salt and pepper

Preheat the oven to 400°F/200°C/Gas Mark 6 and grease a souffle dish with butter.

Bring a saucepan of water to a boil, add the beans, and cook for 5 minutes, or until al dente (tender but still with a bite). Drain and push through a food mill.

Make the béchamel sauce with the ingredients listed (see page 148) and season with salt and pepper.

Stir in the beans, remove from the heat, and stir in the cheese. Cool slightly, then beat in the egg yolks one at a time. Whisk the egg whites to stiff peaks and fold in gently.

Spoon into the prepared dish and bake in the oven for 20 minutes. Lower the oven temperature to 350°F/180°C/Gas Mark 4 and bake for another 5 minutes. Serve immediately.

INDEX

INDEX

Recipe Notes

Butter should always
be unsalted.

Eggs are assumed to be
extra-large (UK: large) size,
unless otherwise specified.

Milk is always full-fat
(whole), unless otherwise
specified.

Cooking and preparation
times are for guidance only,
because individual ovens vary.
If using a convection fan
oven, follow the manufactur-
er's instructions concerning
oven temperatures.

Some recipes include
raw or very lightly cooked
eggs. These should be
avoided particularly by
the elderly, infants, pregnant
women, convalescents,
and anyone with an impaired
immune system.

All spoon measurements
are level. 1 teaspoon = 5 ml;
1 tablespoon = 15 ml. Australian standard tablespoons are
20 ml, so Australian readers
are advised to use 3 teaspoons
in place of 1 tablespoon when
measuring small quantities.

Cup, imperial, and metric
measurements are given
throughout. Follow one set
of measurements, not a mixture, because they are
not interchangeable.

Phaidon Press Limited
Regent's Wharf
All Saints Street
London N1 9PA

Phaidon Press Inc.
65 Bleecker Street
New York, NY 10012

phaidon.com

First published 2016
© 2016 Phaidon Press Limited

ISBN: 978 07148 7122 6

Italian Cooking School Vegetables originates from *Il cucchiaio d'argento*, first published in 1950, eighth edition (revised, expanded, and updated in 1997); *Il cucchiaio d'argento estate*, first published in 2005; *Il cucchiaio d'argento cucina regionale*, first published in 2008; *Scuola di cucina contorni*, first published in 2013. © Editoriale Domus S.p.A. and Cucchiaio s.r.l.

A CIP catalogue record for this book is available from the British Library.

Commissioning Editor: Emilia Terragni
Project Editor: Michelle Meade
Production Controller: Amanda Mackie
Designed by Atlas

Photography © Phaidon Press: Liz and Max Haarala Hamilton 10; Steven Joyce 49, 53, 59, 60, 85, 101, 121, 157, 166, 170, Edward Park 18, 22, 25, 29, 33, 34, 41, 42, 45, 46, 50, 63, 64, 67, 71, 75, 76, 79, 83, 86, 89, 98, 102, 106, 113, 118, 133, 134, 141, 153, 154, 162, 165, 169, 173; Matt Russell 90, 105, 114, 117, 150, 158; Andy Sewell 6, 21, 26, 30, 37, 38, 161

Photography © Editoriale Domus S.p.A. and Cucchiaio d'Argento S.r.l.: Archivio Cucchiaio d'Argento s.r.l. 13, 16, 56, 68, 72, 80, 94, 97, 109, 110, 118, 122, 126, 129, 130, 138, 142, 145, 146, 149

Printed in Romania

The publisher would like to thank Theresa Bebbington, Elizabeth Clinton, Carmen Figini, Lena Hall, Jane Hornby, Ellie Smith, Susan Spaull, Astrid Stavro, and Gemma Wilson for their contributions to the book.